Selections from *The Fancy*.

The Fancy

SELECTIONS

FROM

THE FANCY;

or True Sportsman's Guide.

BY

AN OPERATOR.

———

With a Foreword by
George Plimpton
&
Etching and Drawings by
Randy Jones

———

IMPRINT SOCIETY
BARRE, MASSACHUSETTS
1972

CONTENTS

FOREWORD.

I SHOULD LIKE to make a confession at the start. I under-took the commission of supplying an introduction to this volume of *The Fancy* on the assumption that the research would be relatively straightforward, that I could tell the reader something about the author of the book, his times, which, together with a word or so about pugilism as it was practiced in the Regency period, might whet the appetite of the reader for what follows.

I should have sensed difficulty when I first looked at the original frontispiece—a heraldic design which includes repre-sentations of the various sports offered the reader: a cricket bat, a pit bull, a fighting cock, a boxing ring, a hunting horn, etc.—and discovered that *The Fancy* (or a *True Sports-man's Guide*) had been compiled anonymously by someone referred to as "an operator."

Perhaps there are those whose pulses quicken at such mys-teries, but for me—a sense of woe! But I set to work, and initial research disclosed that "an operator" was generally thought to be one Jonathan Badcock, a writer who (perhaps not unsurprisingly) also wrote under the pseudonym "John Hinds," "John Bee," and often, being a somewhat inconsistent gent, "Jon" Bee.

Whichever, he was apparently one of the foremost sporting journalists during the first decades of the 1800s, though in-deed very little is known about him. In 1811 his *Lives of the Boxers* was issued. That same year he wrote a long preface to a more elaborate volume entitled *Pancratia: a History of Pugilism*, written by Bill Oxberry, who was an actor, journal-ist, and saloon-keeper of the time. Badcock was cashing in on the considerable vogue in pugilism that existed in those days

—an interest undoubtedly due to national pride and a type of English self-assertiveness following the bitter Napoleonic wars. Prize fights were illegal at the time (so proscribed in the courts in 1750) but they were enormously popular, and they enjoyed patronage from such fanciers as the Prince Regent, later King George IV, his brothers, the Duke of York, and the Duke of Clarence, who was later William IV. Indeed, when the Prince of Wales was crowned King on July 24, 1821, eighteen of the leading boxers of England—among them Belcher, Richmond, Cribb, and 'Gentleman' John Jackson (who was Lord Byron's boxing tutor)—acted as ushers at Westminster Hall.

Jonathan Badcock was interested in boxing, doubtless seeing the ring as a colorful, if slightly raunchy slice of English life, but judging from his literary output, his interests obviously ranged to all aspects of that time other than the genteel.

In 1823 Badcock produced a slang dictionary drawn from these various milieus and their splendid wealth of Regency jargon. Its full title page reads: *Slang: A Dictionary of the Turf, the Ring, the Chase, the Pit, of Bon-ton, and the varieties of life, forming an Original and Authentic Lexicon Balatronicum et Macaronicum Particularly Adapted to the Use of THE SPORTING WORLD, for Elucidating Words and Phrases that are necessarily, or purposely, rendered cramp, mutative and unintelligible, outside their respective Spheres. Interspersed with Anecdotes and Whimsies, with tart Quotations and Rum-Ones; with examples proofs and monitory precepts, useful and Proper for NOVICES, FLATS,* and YOKELS.*

In 1818, Badcock had published *Letters from London, Observations of a Russian during Residence in London of* 10 *months,* a book purportedly adapted from an original manuscript by one Olaff Napea, an "ex-officer of the cavalry"—actually a literary device to introduce readers to what was essentially a guidebook to London. In 1828 (under the name Jon Bee) he wrote and published a more straight-forward guide, *A Liv-*

---

* A Flat, according to the definition within, is "one who pays money when he can avoid it . . . he may avoid much evil by studying these pages."

ing Picture of London and Stranger's Guide—which deals largely with what is described on the title page as the 'frauds, the arts, the snares and wiles of . . . rougues that every where abound; with . . . advice how to avoid or defeat their attempts."

As for his interest in pugilism, that continued. In 1826, Badcock issued two volumes entitled *The Fancy* or *A True Sportsman's Guide* (from which this present book is excerpted) which compiles numbers of "the Fancy" publications which began on April 21, 1821.

All of this seems clear enough, except that Badcock had an eminent rival at chronicling this social milieu, indeed one whose name and works are relatively well-known to this day . . . Pierce Egan. A. J. Leibling in his fine book about modern boxing, *The Sweet Science*, refers to Egan as the "greatest writer about the ring who ever lived."

Being a more famous and popular writer of the time, it is easier to come by information about Egan. He was probably born in 1772, died in 1849. He was self-taught, his tastes formed by Shakespeare and 18th century literature, especially Sterne, but his predilections, as were Badcock's, were with the lower orders and their pastimes. His early work appeared in the London *Weekly Dispatch*. In 1811, largely inspired by the great public interest in the two fights between Tom Cribb, the champion, and Tom Molineux, the American black, Pierce Egan began his *Boxiana*, or *Sketches of Pugilism* enterprise, which was eventually to reach five volumes and provide an extraordinary chronicle of that period. Leibling drew upon it with great skill for *The Sweet Science*, relishing its language, and finding comparisons not only between the social behavior of the Regency and today's, but between the character and performance of the fighters separated in time by a century and a half: for example, he finds much in Rocky Marciano's style to compare to that of the Regency's Bill Neat, the Bristol Butcher.

The first volume of *Boxiana* was published anonymously (an infuriating fashion of that time, the reason for which remains obscure to me). Matching Badcock's "an operator,"

Egan titled himself 'one of the Fancy.' He did so for seven years until by popular demand (everyone in London's sporting world already knew and indeed *Blackwood's Edinburgh Magazine* ended a review of the first volume of *Boxiana:* "We see no reason why the author of this celebrated work should remain anonymous any more than the author of *Waverly"*), Egan was finally induced to add his own name to the second volume, which appeared in April, 1818. The cognomens continued to stay with him: "Fancy's Child," "the Great Lexicographer of the Fancy,"* and so forth.

The public acceptance of and enthusiasm over Pierce Egan's *Boxiana* must have outraged Jonathan Badcock. Feeling that his turf was being intruded upon, he reacted strongly. In his 1823 *Slang* dictionary he claims (under the definition of *to Box*) that Egan is not the author of the first volume of *Boxiana* (he allows him the second and third) but credits the publisher, John Smeeton,† for whom both Egan and Badcock had worked as apprentices (Badcock refers to him as "the sixpenny Maecenas of our earliest flights"). Furthermore, much of *Boxiana* (according to Badcock) was derived from *Pancratia,* the Oxberry book for which Badcock had written the introduction. Readers were urged, if they were truly interested in a proper history of the ring, to buy *"The Fancy Chronology; a history of* 700 *battles,* by John (!) Bee, esq. the fancy writer, and present quill man."

The two writers crossed swords again when Pierce Egan became involved, as Badcock had done, in the publication of a slang dictionary. Egan's was actually a revised edition of a popular and well-known work by Francis Grose entitled *The*

---

* A good a time as any to offer a definition of 'the Fancy'—indeed Pierce Egan's own: ". . . any person who is fond of a particular amusement, or closely attached to some subject; a lively instance fortunately presents itself in illustrating the phrase beyond all doubt—as the old lady observed, when she kissed her cat, that it was 'her fancy'."

† In J. C. Reid's excellent biography of Pierce Egan, and of the Regency sporting world, *Bucks and Bruisers* (published in England in 1971) this Smeeton turns up as 'George'—described by Professor Reid as one of the most imaginative and successful of the popular publishers of the early 1800s, his output ranging from the *Eccentric Magazine* (in which were described the lives of freaks) to more respectable volumes such as *Biographia Curiosa* or *Memoirs of Remarkable Characters of the Reign of George III* (1822). 'John' or 'George,' take your pick.

Classical Dictionary of the Vulgar Tongue, which first appeared in 1785. What Pierce did was to update Grose's definitions, offer some of his own (about a sixth of the book), and add part of a treatise called *Lexicon Balatronicum: A Dictionary of Buckish Slang, University Wit, and Pickpocket Eloquence.* His volume came out a year in advance of Badcock's (in 1822); Badcock was not only extremely critical of it, but contended that Egan had heard about a rival dictionary being put together, and had rushed ahead with a quick collation to get his out first, and other than editing someone else's work had not done much more than add a few "inventions of the editor's own manufacture."

In fact, it is great fun to dip into both dictionaries. Egan's is perhaps the fuller (he does, after all, combine material from other authorities) and livelier (some of the racier words he defines have just found their way into contemporary dictionaries), and has been credited with being the source for any number of Victorian novelists looking for authentic language. But this is not to slight Badcock's dictionary. I was especially taken by his definition of what is referred to as 'an Exquisite'—*"another name for Dandy, but of a more refined or feminine manner. The* Chronicle *says, "It is a fact that an* Exquisite *fainted away on Friday, Dec. 20th, in Bond-street, and was assisted into a shop, where he remained some time before he recovered. Medical aid being sent for, it was ascertained that his valet had laced his stays too tight."*

Badcock's sniping at Egan did not end with the dictionary squabble. In 1820, four years after Badcock had published his *Letters from London, Observations of a Russian,* etc., his rival published *Life in London,* or to give it its full title, *Life in London, or the Day and Night Sprees of Jerry Hawthorn Esq. and his Elegant friend Corinthian Tom, accompanied by Bob Logic, the Oxonian, in their Rambles and Sprees through the Metropolis.* The book was an enormous success, far outstripping Badcock's effort, despite the latter's criticism of it: "Lies, lies, lies, from beginning to end . . . false as Hell, and ugly as Hecate."

Egan's book (its success caused him to be presented at the

court of George IV) spawned a number of imitations. The best of them was *Real Life in London; or the Rambles and Adventures of Bob Tallyho, Esq. and his cousin, the Hon. Tom Dashall, through the Metropolis*. It is written with enough elan and sophistication so that some authorities have ascribed it to Egan, though he himself called the work, "a bare-faced piracy." A more possible candidate is our friend, Jonathan Badcock, fighting back as best he could, although, despite opportunities to do so, he never acknowledged the book's authorship.

The two writers became involved yet once again. In 1823 Pierce Egan got in touch with the publishers of *Boxiana* (Sherwood, Neely and Jones) and told them that he wished to publish the fourth volume on his own. The publishers took him to court on the grounds that since they held the copyright, he could not use the name *Boxiana* for his own purposes. The publishers lost the case, the court finding that Egan was fully entitled, as author of the first three volumes, to continue writing the work on his own behalf. The court's decision did not seem to deter the publishers from continuing the *Boxiana* series on their own. In 1824, Sherwood, Neely and Jones published a fourth volume of *Boxiana*, announcing at the time that ". . . the Proprietor takes occasion to allude to the change which it has been necessary to make in the editorship of the preceding volume. In making these changes, they have been induced to avail themselves of a gentleman of good practical knowledge and judgement on all parts of the subject, whereby they have been enabled to introduce much improvement, both in the plan and execution of the work."

Who should the new editor be, almost without question, but Jonathan Badcock. Not only was he responsible for Vol. IV, but he revised the earlier volumes from 1824 onwards, so that Egan's authentic text is actually only to be found in editions of *Boxiana* published pre-1824. In post-1824 editions, the *Fancy* finds its way into the *Boxiana* lexicon, and in some editions parts of the *Fancy* are bound into Vol. III.

As for Pierce Egan's fourth volume, he finally got it out four years later, in 1828. It was dedicated to the Earl of Eldon who had decided for him in the court case with Sherwood, Neely and Jones, and was entitled *New Series of Boxiana*. Within was the warning: "Beware of Imposters. Foul Fighters are in the Field."

All of this leads up to an uncomfortable admission on my part that I cannot tell the reader which author—Egan or Badcock—he will be reading in the pages which follow.

The volume leads off with a remarkable history of boxing (it's actually entitled *Cursory Remarks on the Origins, Rise, and Progress, of Pugilism in England*) which has always been attributed to Egan. It begins the first volume of *Boxiana* (Badcock would thus attribute it to Smeeton) and appears under Egan's name in a short treatise entitled *A Lecture on the Art of Self-Defense* (1845). But the contributions to the rest of the book are more difficult. Judging from what I take to be original sources, both Egan's and Badcock's accounts of the fighter, Joshua Hudson, say, are identical. On the other hand, both write quite differently about Jack Martin, though on occasion a phrase will be identical (it must be remembered that in this period writers borrowed and plagiarized shamelessly). Occasionally, one writer, then the other, will pepper a phrase to give it more life. Here are the two authors writing about Tom Molineux.

Badcock: "Molineux's first *set-to* in England was with a Bristol man, of robust make, and about six feet in height, in Tothill-fields."

Egan: "He had no high sounding name as a patron to *eclat* his entrée, and he *peeled* for the first time on British ground on July 24, 1810, against a Bristol man of robust make, and about six feet in height, in Tothill Field."

Egan obviously does more with this material but in essence, both writers' styles are alike—racy, energetic, rhetorical, full of literary allusion, with Badcock less endowed with wit, and certainly less generous with his need to capitalize and italicize words. In sum, Badcock must be considered the editor of *The Fancy*, and how fine his own hand in the contributions he includes, whether as editor or author, is not an easy matter to discern.

A word about this volume itself. The original *The Fancy* consisted of two volumes, which were published in 1828. The 'operator' included not only boxing "memoires," but also a portion on feats of "pedestrianism" (which was a popular pastime of the era), and an additional section entitled "miscellaneous." The present volume has been pruned in all departments, with the pedestrian accounts, which are mostly statistics, left out entirely. The 'miscellaneous' section was difficult to cut since the index of the original sparkles with headings that pique the reader's curiosity. Such items (usually running to a paragraph or so in length in the text) are listed in the index under such headings as: *Mr. J. Streeter, eats 20 boiled eggs in 5 minutes*; *the Boa Constrictor and the Goat*; *Sagacity of a Hedge Hog*; *a Bride married in her Chemise*; *Extraordinary Fecundity of a Ewe*; *Gallantry of an Elephant, etc.*

Surely (one might say) these contributions must be Badcock's own. Not at all. Pierce Egan was the author of such a Collection (*Sporting Anecdotes*, 1825) and many of the items, if one compares, are identical. The accounts of the Boa Constrictor and the Goat (hardly a contest; the goat loses decisively) are the same in both volumes. So is the text which describes the 'sagacious' hedgehog.

But then obviously the value of these pages from *The Fancy* does not depend on the identity of the author. Whoever he is, he pales beside the strong portraits of the great pugilists described—Bob Whitaker; Nat Peartree; Tom Cribb, the Black Diamond; Jean Belcher; John Francis, the Jumping Soldier; Harry Gray, the Clog Maker; or Thomas Hickman, the Gas-Light Man, who against George Cooper, the Bargeman, ". . . came in contact with a tip of his antagonist's nose, and drawing the cartilage by a side twist so as to dislocate the integuments a good way around, occasioned a great internal extravasation of blood."

In his introduction to *The Fancy* the "operator" states what he wishes to achieve: "to give admirers of the Fancy, residing at a distance, a proper notion of the times we live in, but a faithful and luminous display of whatever is passing worthy of notice, in the metropolis particularly, altogether forming such a meanful chronicle, and panoramic assemblage of Fancy sports, as will enable the future historian to appreciate properly

"The taste and manners of the times
And give to every age its shape and dignity"

"Come, Reader! Let us *shake hands*" is the opening exhortatory epigram to the volume. I am all for it—whether we are to shake hands with Egan, or Badcock, or Hinds, or Bee (Jon or John), or even George (or is it John?) Smeeton.

GEORGE PLIMPTON

Selections from *The Fancy*.

INTRODUCTION.

Come, Reader! "let us *shake hands*."

Nothing like this publication on *Fancy Sports* has ever before been printed: in some particular point or other it differs from every one of its predecessors, and in nothing so much as in the *manner* of execution, its faithfulness and variety being as yet unequalled. Whilst it professes to

"Eye nature's walks, shoot folly as it flies,
"And catch the manners living as they rise,"

in all the varied sports connected with Pugilism, a due regard will be had to the more serious, moral, and instructive lessons to be derived from its practice. Nay, Reader, be not startled! this promise will be verified *in the sequel*; for we shall not pounce upon such dry inferences at once,—like a hen jumping at a blackberry,—but will lead thee round and round thy favorite bush, beating the cover, until at length we start the game, and expose it to the view judgmatically.

The character of the ring was exalted by such men as Humphries and Gully, but never could receive a *grace* from Buckhorse, or his successors, nor be disgraced by the errors of the Young Ruffian, Bourke, or Dick; but *'tis disgraced* when the smaller aberrations of such men, and of some others now alive, are either passed silently over, if not *lauded*, instead of being reprobated, repressed, or otherwise discouraged, by our writers on Pugilism, forsooth: they know not, poor scribes, how much influence their very silence has on the minds of men whose understandings lie in their heels, whose greatest wit is to be found at their knuckle-ends. We mean no disparagement of the otherwise-gifted; for we happen to know many fighting-men who are tolerable reasoners, and remember well, that one of the three characters just named is a good grammar scholar, and once won a wager, made with *one of us*, on a question purely literary. "No hard matter," say you: but *Ne bocklish*, man.

YOUR ATTENTION will be directed occasionally to the practice of boxing in the olden time, when it began to supersede, or made part of the study, of feats of arms; deducing it thence to the present era, when the exercise of Pugilism as an art, having superseded the use of *such arms*, and received the royal assent, when you shall find it reducible to rules, and every blow of importance can be satisfactorily accounted for. This will be the course we shall pursue, as soon as the pressure of temporary matters of fact, leaves a page or two in each number at leisure for precepts, which will be founded on experience, and advice that must not be neglected, by the aspirant after fisty honours. But whilst we keep in view, throughout our work, the inculcation of the genuine Art of Self-Defence, and the love of Manly Sports, no less will it embrace the wide field of forceful exertion of all animated nature, from a *horse-race* to a *maggot-match*, and from a *monkey-scratch* to a *man-fight*; without forgetting what is due to the best of human feelings, or the decent and orderly conduct of those who exhibit for the public amusement and instruction. Our prime delight will be to induce the Readers of "THE FANCY" to think more highly of *man* and his achievements, his capabilities and superiority to other animals—to say no more. Great care will likewise be taken to record every occurrence that transpires, in the Ring, or out of it, regarding our *bipedal* exertions; whilst a *selection* only from the performances of the *all-four going* part of the creation (quadrupeds) will be narrated, from time to time; but these shall include the *best-done things* of their kind, so arranged as to give the admirers of THE FANCY, residing at a distance, a proper notion of the times we live in, by a faithful and luminous display of whatever is passing worthy of notice, in the metropolis particularly.

Altogether forming such a manful chronicle, and panoramic assemblage of FANCY SPORTS, as will enable the future historian to appreciate properly:

> "The taste and manners of the times;
> "And give to every age its shape and dignity."

The Publisher would not have offered the present publication to the notice of THE RING, and its admirers, nor attempted to draw upon them, fortnightly, for the price of a pot of *heavy wet*, to keep the game alive, if he could have persuaded himself that their attention was already adequately occupied by the present miserably defective *slummery mode* of bringing these matters upon the carpet. A mode whereby *froth* is served up for the *substance, epithet* stands in the stead of *sense*, and a constantly feverish state of risible ridiculousness is foisted off for understanding. Besides these *just* objections to the *manner* in which this species of subjects has been hitherto mismanaged, we complain that an inflated pomposity has been imposed upon us for sublimity, tameness for accuracy, flippancy for liveliness, and turgidity for precision—a *state of things* this which could not always last; and if we do no other good,

> " 'Twill put them 'pon their mettle."

But we look a little higher than this comes to: although we know full well that few among *'the men'* are grammarians, —all round the ring you shall not find a critic; that some one here and there does not choose to read at all, whilst a good number seldom *spell right*, in book or out of it; nor does either the one or the other "signify a bunch of cat's meat;" but it does signify a good deal (and here is the *sore*) that Mr. ——— nor ——— should be longer permitted to go about *teaching* those things *wrongfully*, without being told of it, tidily, as we do now.

A vast difference exists between people *falling* into errors of this nature, and being *dragged*, or *led*, into them, by flowery paths and devious ways; for, be it remembered, that "men are led by the nose more than by the understanding," in matters of mind connected with FANCY SPORTS particularly. For our parts we would, at any time, rather instruct the mind and amend the heart of any man than meddle with his *konk*.

Moreover, let us say, we hope we never shall act "like that pharisee," nor "scribble like that scribe." [*Juvenal*] On the contrary, we propose to keep ourselves entirely free from prejudices, from party attachments, and from sycophancy of every kind; from fawning over a conqueror, or becoming a lick-spittle to a lord, whether that be a *peer-lord*, or a *landlord:* from lauding a man for his infamies, because he happens to be *up*, or treading on another because he is *down* in the world; —well recollecting that many a good man who has gone up, up, up, in the public estimation, is now "down, down, down-a," in the ring, as well as out of it.

A FEW preliminary general explanations will be found in the earlier numbers, not altogether the most interesting, perhaps, to those who may be *"down as a hammer* to every thing;" but which were absolutely necessary for duly understanding the subsequent pages, by those who may not be *fly* to so much as they.

CURSORY REMARKS

ON

The Origin, Rise, and Progress,

OF

Pugilism in England.

IT is far from our intention, by way of apology, to prove that Pugilism is of an ancient date in reference to the Greeks and Romans, and that it was sanctioned by these distinguished nations, in their public sports, and in the education of youth, to manifest its utility in strengthening the body, dissipating all fear, and infusing a manly courage into the system.

We shall, therefore, view it as a national propensity, independent of every other consideration; and that Pugilism is in perfect unison with the feeling of Englishmen; references to dates, if necessary, will bear us out. Distinction of rank is of little importance when an offence has been given, and in the impulse of the moment, a Prince has forgotten his royalty, by turning out to box, to prevent the imputation of a coward—a Duke, his consequence in life—and a Bishop, the sanctity of his cloth; displaying those strong and *national* traits so congenial to the soil of liberty.

No men are more subject to the caprice or changes of fortune than the pugilists; *victory* brings them fame, riches, and patrons; their bruises are not heeded in the smiles of success; and, basking in the sunshine of prosperity, their lives pass on pleasantly, till *defeat* comes and reverses the scene: covered with aches and pains, distressed in mind and body, assailed by poverty, wretchedness, and misery,—friends forsake them— their towering fame expired—their characters suspected by

[7]

losing—they fly to inebriation for relief, and a premature end puts a period to their misfortunes.

It is one of the greatest failings of human nature, incident to most men in every station of society, that while in prosperity, and a long run of good luck, few are provident enough to provide against a rainy day; much more from those who are in a line of life, where a great deal depends upon *chance*, and an unlucky throw may reduce them considerably worse than their first outset in life; a memorable instance is to be remarked toward strengthening this argument, respecting the late Tom Johnson, of pugilistic celebrity, who, by his extraordinary success in fighting, it is said had realized the astonishing sum of near 5,000 pounds; and might, after contending for the championship of England, in about sixteen fights, have retired from the scene of "battles bravely fought and hardly won," into the vale of ease, become respectable, and have ended his days in peace and happiness. But by want of conduct he lost his property and his home; *necessity* compelled him to fight another battle; and, flattered that the *chance* was still in his favour, whereby he might recruit his exhausted finances, he entered the field with all the gaiety of an adventurer; but, alas! capricious fortune turned her back upon him, and he, who had always been borne off upon the shoulders of his friends, amid the shouts of victory, was now doomed, O dire reverse! by the desperate conflict he had sustained, to *give in*; the laurel torn from his veteran brow, and death, the ultimate consequence, from the severe blows he had received.

Boxing, at any rate, has been patronized for upwards of seventy years in England; and among its numerous leaders several of the Blood Royal have stood conspicuous, towards its support, independent of Dukes, Lords, Honourables, &c. &c.

But what of that! have not our classic theatres, within the last five-and-twenty years possessing all the advantages of authors the most exalted and refined; actors the most inimitable and chaste, either to extort the tear or provoke the laugh; music the most ravishing; scenes and decorations, in point of magnificence and splendour, unparalleled—invited Pugilism to their boards, and the names of some of the first rate boxers enriched their playbills; and the audiences (of whom no doubt can attach to their respectability) testified their approbation by loud plaudits, at the liberality of the managers in thus publicly displaying the principles of Pugilism! And it is mentioned upon good authority, that the most fashionable daily newspaper of that period, under the direction of an *amateur* captain, had a rapid increase of sale, in respect to its containing the genuine correspondence between those celebrated heroes of the fist—Humphries and Mendoza.

In 1791 Pugilism was in such high repute, and so strongly patronized, that Dan Mendoza was induced to open the small theatre, at the Lyceum, in the Strand, for the express purpose of public exhibitions of sparring; and, in his managerial capacity, assured the public, by a neat and appropriate address, that the manly art of boxing would be displayed, divested of all ferocity, rendered equally as neat and elegant as fencing, perfectly as useful, and might be as gracefully acquired. Several imitations would be given of celebrated ancient and modern pugilists; eminent performers were engaged to pourtray the science; and the whole conducted with the utmost propriety and decorum, that the female part of the creation might attend, without their feelings being infringed upon, or experiencing any unpleasant sensations.

About this period, a similar exhibition was opened, near the Haymarket, under the guidance of a Frenchman, who undertook to prove that *science,* in competition with *strength,* was of no avail; but *John Bull* soon took the *conceit* out of him, as he had done many more of his countrymen, in more formidable contests than that of *sparring,* by exposing his *gasconade.* The Frenchman very soon got *milled,* and, shortly afterwards, *mizzled;* so that the science received but little interruption from *his* lectures on the gymnastic art.

In illustration of *Boxing* being a national and important feature of the English people, we relate the following anecdote of an illustrious personage:—

The late Lord B—— (the firm of that *elegant* family quartette, knowingly styled, Newgate, Hellgate, Cripplegate, and Billingsgate) about the year 1789, was in the very zenith

of his fun, frolic, and *lark-ery*; and, if we *can believe* his Lordship's panegyrist, he was notwithstanding his volatile propensities, a man of observation and talent; and *correct* in music,
if nothing else. No *milling* match of note his lordship ever
missed, but he always was conspicuous in the scene; and the
lessons he had received, under the first-rate professors of the
art, rendered him no mean adept in the science. Though he
performed in public on the classic stage, we never heard that
he had ever sported his *Corinthian canvass* as a pugilist in the
open ring; but was fond of kicking up a *row*, and not afraid to
fight his way out of it. He was a public character in the extreme
at Brighton; and his eccentricities at that watering place will
not be easily forgotten. In one of his wild freaks, unfortunately,
he horse-whipped from his phaëton a respectable perfumer, (a
Mr. Donadieu, who was in a gig,) for not getting out of his
way: his Lordship's thorough bred cattle soon distanced the
man of scent, before he could well recover from his surprise;
but, the next morning, Mr. D. perceiving Lord B——— upon
the Steine, in company with several sporting men, pugilists,
&c. went up to him and remonstrated on the ill-usage he had
received upon the preceding day, when his lordship, instead
of redressing, set about *milling* him for his insolence; but the
perfumer being an Englishman, and not feeling dismayed by
the superior rank of his antagonist, and having a good *pluck*,
quickly returned the *favour* with interest; his Lordship soon
perceived he was on a *wrong scent*, that not only his *fame*, as a
pugilist, was at stake, but his honour, as a peer, in danger of
being wounded, and began to take an unfair advantage, when
the P——— of W———, who had witnessed the whole
transaction from a window at the pavilion, exclaimed, with all
the native characteristic of a Briton *"Dam'me B——— fight
like a man!"*

DUELLING—however honourable and proper such a mode
of settling differences may be considered; we confess, that we
are no advocates for such a *genteel* system; notwithstanding
cowardice must be despised, and urge that no man ought to
put up with a gross insult or unprovoked injury pusillani-
mously. The laws of honour, doubtless, are of so fine and

delicate a texture, that they are not to be grasped at by every rough hand, nor to be referred to upon all occasions; but the *ridiculous appeals*, which have been made, in too many instances, to those sacred laws, forcibly bring to recollection, that, in such cases, it is "a custom more honoured in the breach than in the observance."

Man from the imperfections of his nature, is liable to quarrel, and to give or receive insults in his journey through life—how necessary, then, does it appear that he should be able to defend himself—and that in a way which will bear reflection. The fastidious, we have little doubt, will smile at the phrase—*reflection*; but how much misery and wretchedness might have been spared by that reflection, of the dreadful consequences likely to arise from *duelling*—in making their wives premature and unprovided widows; their children fatherless and distressed; and themselves snatched away in a moment, with all their imperfections on their head, and reconciliation put out of the question. If it were possible to take a peep into the *penetralia* of those persons who go out to decide quarrels after this *genteel* mode, we rather apprehend, that, in deciding with truth, something like *fear* might be perceived at the bottom, if all-powerful honour did not prevent its having a resting place!

Where, *then*, is the relative, however high in pride and pomp, on viewing the father, husband, or brother, killed in a duel—but what would rather that they should have had recourse to the manly defence of *Boxing*, than the deadly weapons of sword and ball; from which a bloody nose, or black eye, might have been the only consequences to themselves, and their families, and neither in their feelings or their circumstances been injured; reconciliation with their antagonist—faults mutually acknowledged—and, perhaps, become inseparable friends ever afterwards.

We have long witnessed the good effects of this manly spirit in England; and, we trust, it will never be extinguished. Prejudice does much in favour of our native soil; but, upon a dispassionate review of those countries where Pugilism is unknown, we find, that, upon the most trifling misunderstanding, the life of the individual is in danger. In Holland the long knife decides too frequently; scarcely any person in Italy is without the stiletto; and France and Germany are not particular in using stones, sticks, &c. to gratify revenge; but, in England, the *fist* only is used, where malice is not suffered to engender and poison the composition, and induce the inhabitants to the commission of deeds which their souls abhor and shudder at.

It has been attempted, by some writers, to prove that *boxing* did not originate in Great Britain; but in recurring to the times of the immortal Alfred, according to ancient authorities, we shall find, that *wrestling* and *boxing* formed a part of the manual exercise of the soldiers at that distant period. The ancient Britons have always been characterised as a manly, strong, and robust race of people, inured to hardship and fatigue, and, by the exercise of those manly sports, acquired that peculiar *strength of arm*, which rendered them so decisive in their warlike combats.

And, were it materially necessary, the curious Old English Sports might be traced through the succeeding reigns, with every degree of certainty, except in some few instances, where the conquerors introduced *effeminate refinements*, of which Leland and several other historians speak, as tending towards creating a degeneracy of spirit among the natives of the island.

It appears that Richard III. (commonly denominated *crook-backed* Richard) was distinguished for his acquirements of those exercises which invigorated the body and strengthened the arm; and it is recorded of him, "that he was uncommonly expert, either on foot or horseback, in displaying a variety of manly feats,—such as drawing the bow, raising the sling, or throwing the javelin; but particularly distinguished with a *clenched fist*, when opposed to an antagonist, by the extreme potency of his arm." In those days it was expected, that *even* princes should excel in these necessary and manly accomplishments, as much depended upon the power of the *arm*;—and however *high-colouring* it may give to stage effect, in witnessing Richard fall in the contest with Richmond—had that have proved the fact, that the fate of the nation was to have been decided by a single combat, the superiority of Richard's prowess, by his being inured to feats of manhood, and the various hardy exploits he had performed, little doubt can be expressed, but Richmond would never have assumed the kingly title of Henry VII. Richard's natural courage was of the first order; and, in the words of our immortal bard, finely expressed:—

> "I think there be six Richmonds in the field
> "Five have I slain to day instead of him."

————o◯o————

Having thus far cursorily expressed our opinions in favour of this manly art, we shall now proceed to shew some of its most powerful *knock-down* arguments:—

Jack Broughton, according to the best authorities, appears to have been considered as the Father of the English School of Boxing, and by whose superior skill and ability Pugilism obtained the rank of a Science.

Previous to the days of Broughton it was downright *slaughtering,*—or, in the modern acceptation, either *gluttony, strength,* or *bottom,* decided almost every contest. But, after Broughton appeared as a professor of the gymnastic art, he drew crowds after him to witness his exhibitions; there was a *neatness* about his method completely new and unknown to his auditors—he *stopped* the blows aimed at any part of him by his antagonist, with so much skill, and *hit* his man away with so much ease, that he astonished and terrified his opponents beyond measure; and those persons who had the temerity to enter the lists with him were soon convinced of his superior knowledge and athletic prowess: and most of his competitors, who were compelled to *give in,* from their exhausted and beaten state, had the mortification to behold Broughton scarcely touched, and to appear with as much cheerfulness and indifference as if he had never been engaged in a *set-to.*

Notwithstanding the inferiority of Boxers, previous to the days of Broughton, it may not be improper, as far as they can be traced with any degree of accuracy, so as to render the connection more complete and strong, to give some short account of their feats.

Southwark Fair, during its continuance, was an uncommon scene of attraction to the inhabitants in, and contiguous to

London, from the various sports and pastimes which were exhibited by its versatility of performers. Boxing and cudgelling were strong features among the other amusements: refinement, it appears, was not so well understood *then* as at the present period.

Nor did that Colossus of Literature (Dr. Johnson) appear shy, in witnessing the eccentricities developed by human beings at such places of amusement, where the finest display of *nature* and *art* that could be experienced were to be seen *contrasted*, and *real life*, in all its abundant varieties, pourtrayed in its native dress. To a *mind* like that of Dr. Johnson's, few circumstances escaped his notice, whether attracted by the loud laugh at the rude and noisy fair, or the *self-approving* smile at the more refined and splendid chateau; in the manly display of the pugilist or in appealing eloquence of the orator, it was appreciated and treasured up, added to his midnight sallies with the unfortunate and pitiable Savage, united with his intellectual acquirements; and which, doubtless, formed the *stamina* of those works that have tended to add so much literary reputation to this country.

The learned Doctor, in himself, was another *striking* proof of pugilism being a national trait, by having a regular set-to with an athletic brewer's servant, who had insulted him in Fleet-street, and gave the fellow a complete milling in a few minutes.

Boxing and *cudgelling*, it appeared, degenerated into downright ferocity and barbarity, at this fair, from the drunkenness and inequality of the combatants, and the various artifices adopted to get money, which at last became so disgusting, that it was declared a public nuisance, and in 1743 Southwark fair was suppressed.

It was from the above scene of frolic and fun, that the inimitable Hogarth drew his celebrated picture of Southwark Fair, in which life is exhibited in all its various shapes from the King to the Beggar; and among the variety of characters here pourtrayed, may be traced the likenesses of the late King, interestedly gazing upon the rude and comic touches of nature, and in viewing the merry countenances of his happy subjects, enjoying the humours and freedom of their countrymen, so congenial to the soil of liberty; and the famous Colly Cibber, of theatrical fame, in observing the display of talent, sported by his brethren of the *sock* and *buskin* to the gaping crowd, to persuade the populace to fill their booths, that they might *begin immediately*; and the heroic Figg, of pugilistic memory, challenging any one of the crowd to enter the lists with him, either for money, for love, or a bellyfull!

The latter character, at this period, was a distinguished personage in the history of pugilism, by references being made to him upon all fighting occasions; and was considered to possess good judgment. He might be looked upon as the champion of that day.—Figg was more indebted to strength and courage for his success in the battles which he gained, than from the effects of genius: in fact, he was extremely illiterate, and it might be said he *boxed* his way through life. If Figg's method of fighting was subject to the *criticism* of the present day, he would be denominated more of a *slaughterer* than that of a neat, finished pugilist. His antagonists were punished severely in their conflicts with him, particularly those who stood up to receive his blows; in making matches his advice was always consulted, as he possessed the character of an honest fellow— and was looked up to as a leading fighter among the most distinguished of the *fancy*.

It appears that Fig was more distinguished as a *fencer* and *cudgeller* than as a pugilist; and, notwithstanding the former acquirements gave him a decidedly superior advantage over the other boxers of that day, by his thorough acquaintance with *time* and *measure*, yet his favourite practices were the *sword* and *stick*, and in the use of which he particularly excelled.

His reputation rapidly increasing as a scientific man in those pursuits, he was induced to open an amphitheatre for teaching the use of the small and back-sword, cudgelling, and pugilism; and which place soon became of considerable notoriety, by proving a great attraction to the sporting men at that period, in making and settling matches in the various bouts that were displayed.

It was here that the celebrated Captain Godfrey (the *Bar-*

clay of that time) displayed his uncommon skill and elegance in those manly sports, with the most hardy and determined competitors, contending for the palm of victory; and often was the Captain witnessed by royal and noble personages, whom, it should seem, became supporters to a science, tending to inure the people to bravery and intrepidity.

To Captain Godfrey's *Treatise upon the useful Science of Defence*, (now extremely scarce,) published in 1747, we are, in some degree, indebted for an account of the characters of the *Fancy* within his time. Which work was dedicated to his Royal Highness the Duke of Cumberland, and was so well received by the public, that it immediately went through two large editions.

The Captain thus speaks of Fig:—"I have purchased my knowledge with many a broken head, and bruises in every part of me. I chose to go mostly to Fig, and exercise with him; partly, as I knew him to be the ablest master, and, partly, as he was of a rugged temper, and would spare no man, high or low, who took up a stick against him. I bore his rough treatment with determined patience, and followed him so long, that Fig, at last, finding he could not have the beating of me at so cheap a rate as usual, did not shew such fondness for my company. This is well known by gentlemen of distinguished rank, who used to be pleased in setting us together."

It was about this period, that the whole boxing hemisphere was *up in arms!* occasioned by the *insolent* threats of the English laurels being torn from their native soil, and transplanted to a foreign land!—It was a *Venetian* Gondolier that *threw down the glove*, boasting, at the same time, that he would break the jaw-bone of any opponent who might have the temerity to fight him. The *Venetian* was a man of prodigious strength, possessing an *arm* not only very large and muscular, but surprisingly long; and had proved a complete terror to his own countrymen, by the number of *jaw-bones* which he had sent to the surgeons to be *set*, of those persons who had possessed hardihood enough to oppose him. His fame ran before him, and his impetuosity was described to be irresistible. The *Venetian* was considered a good subject for winning, and a foreigner of distinction and several of his countrymen backed him for a large sum;—but John Bull was not thus to be *bounced* out of his *pluck* or his money—and, in this situation of affairs, Fig was applied to for a customer to *serve him out,* if such a one could be found!—"Found," exclaimed Fig, laughing heartily, "aye, my Masters, plenty; but I don't know, d'ye see, as how that'ere's truth about his breaking so many of his countrymen's jaw-bones with his fist; howsomedever, that's no matter, he can't break Bob Whitaker's jaw-bone, if he had a sledge-hammer in his hand. And if Bob must knock under, why, before this here *outlandish* waterman shall rule the roast, I'll give him a Fig to *chaw,* which, perhaps, he'll find some trouble in *swallowing!"* After this luminous display upon the matter, the match was made, and the day appointed for the combat, to take place at Fig's Amphitheatre.

It may be necessary to say something here about the qualifications of Bob Whitaker, who was selected to *punish* this *Venetian* for his vain-boasting, that he would take *the shine out* of Englishmen! Bob was an awkward boxer, and an athletic man; but possessed true *bottom,* and was celebrated for his throwing, and contriving to pitch his weighty body on his fallen antagonist.

Among the *milling coves* the day was looked for with uncommon anxiety, that was to decide this mighty contest:—

"When Greek meets Greek, then comes the tug of war."

The important moment at length arrived, and, according to all report, it was by far the most splendid company, and the politest house of the kind that was ever seen at Fig's Amphitheatre.

The stage was ordered to be cleared, when an awful silence prevailed in the anxiety manifested for the *set-to.* The *Venetian* mounted with smiles of confidence, and was greeted welcome by loud plaudits from his countrymen and partisans, and instantly began to strip—his *giant-like arm* claimed universal astonishment, and his size in general struck terror, and even Captain Godfrey observes, "That his heart yearned for his countryman!" Bob appeared cool and steady, in a few seconds afterwards, and was cheered with huzzas. He eyed the Gondolier with firmness, and quite undismayed, threw off his clothes in an instant, when the attack commenced,—the *Venetian* pitched himself forward with his right leg, and his arm full extended, and, before Whitaker was aware of his design, he received a blow on the side of the head, so powerful in its effect, as to *capsize* him over the stage, which was remarkable for its height. Whitaker's fall was desperate indeed, as he dashed completely against the ground; which circumstance would not have taken place, but for the grandeur of the audience, whose prices for admission were so high on that day as to exclude the common people, who generally sat on the ground, and formed a line around the stage. It was then all clear, and Bob had nothing to stop him but the bottom. The bets ran high, and the foreigners vociferated loudly indeed in behalf of the *Venetian*, and flattered themselves that Whitaker would scarcely be able to *come again* from the desperate blow and fall that he had received, and sported their cash freely in laying the odds thick against him; but Bob was not to be *told out* so soon, and jumped upon the stage, like a game-cock to renew the attack. *Sparring* was now all at an end; and Whitaker found out that something must be done to render the *Venetian's long arm* useless, or he must lose the fight; so, without further ceremony, he made a little stoop, and ran boldly in beyond the heavy mallet, and with one *"English peg"* in the stomach, (quite a new thing to foreigners,) brought him on his breech. The tables were then turned, the sporting men laughing heartily, and the foreigners a little chop-fallen. The *Venetian* showed symptoms of uneasiness—was quite sick—and his wind being touched, he was scarcely to his *time*. Bob now *punished* him in fine style, drove the *Venetian* all over the stage, and soon gave him a *leveller*. The odds shifted fast in favour of Whitaker, and the foreigners displayed some terrible *long faces!* The Gondolier was completely puzzled, and, in the course of a few rounds, the *conceit was so taken out of him*, that he lost all guard of his person, and was compelled to *give in*—to the no small chagrin of the foreigners, who were properly *cleaned out* upon this occasion; but the *Venetian* had the mortification to retire in disgrace, after his vain-boasting, and with a good *milling*; or, as Captain Godfrey concludes, "the blow in the stomach carried too much of the English *rudeness* for him to bear, and finding himself so unmannerly used, he scorned to have any more doings with his slovenly fist."

Fig was so enraptured with the elegance of the audience, and not wishing to let so good an opportunity slip, instantly mounted the stage, and addressed the spectators, nearly to the following purport:—"Gentlemen, perhaps, as how, you may think, that I have picked out the best man in London to beat this here foreigner; but if you will come this day se'nnight, I'll produce a man that shall beat Bob Whitaker, by fair hitting, in ten minutes."—It had the desired effect, by the company proving as great and as fine as the week before, and who came to see whether Fig was not trifling with them; it being considered a difficult task to beat such a *bottom* man as Whitaker in so short a space of time. On the day appointed, the Amphitheatre, as before, was crowded at an early hour, and poor Whitaker's laurels were doomed to be but of short duration. Nat Peartree was the man looked out to deprive him of his honours; and who was considered a most admirable Boxer; and had he not lost a finger in a desperate conflict, it was supposed that Peartree was a match for any of the pugilists. He was famous for fighting at the face, and putting in his blows with great strength; yet felt doubtful in being able to beat Whitaker by force, as the latter had proved himself, upon many occasions, a most enormous *glutton*, and therefore cunningly determined to fight at his eyes. The event proved Peartree's judgment to be correct, for, in about six minutes, he had directed his arms so well, that Whitaker was shut out from day-light, by both his eyes being closed up. In this *distressed* situation he became an object of pity, by being completely at the mercy of his antagonist; when poking about awhile, for his man, and finding him not, he wisely gave in, with these odd words—"Dam'me, I am not beat, but what signifies when I cannot see my man!"

The time was at length arrived, when Fig, notwithstanding his celebrated parryings, and severe thrusts, was doomed to meet with a superior antagonist—and *Death* gave him his *knock-down-blow* in 1740.

About this year, public challenges of the Pugilists were advertised; and at the various Fairs hand-bills were distributed of their feats to be displayed; and, endeavouring to make as complete a book of reference as possible, we are induced to insert the following specimens:—

AT

FIG'S GREAT TIL'D BOOTH,

On the Bowling-Green, Southwark,

During the time of the *FAIR*,

(Which begins on SATURDAY, the 18th of SEPTEMBER)

The TOWN will be entertained with the

MANLY ARTS OF

Foil-play, Back-sword, Cudgelling, and Boxing,

in which

The noted PARKS, from Coventry, and the celebrated gentleman prize-fighter, Mr. MILLAR, will display their skill in a tilting-bout, shewing the advantages of *Time* and *Measure*:

ALSO

Mr. JOHNSON, the great Swordsman, superior to any man in the World for his unrivalled display of the *hanging-guard*, in a grand attack of SELF-DEFENCE, against the all-powerful arm of the renowned SUTTON.

DELFORCE, the finished Cudgeller, will likewise exhibit his uncommon feats with the *single-stick*; and who challenges any man in the kingdom to enter the lists with him for a *broken-head* or a *belly-full!*

BUCKHORSE, and several other *Pugilists*, will shew the art of Boxing.

To conclude

With a GRAND PARADE by the valiant FIG, who will exhibit his knowledge in various combats—with the Foil, Back-sword, Cudgel, and Fist.

To begin each Day at Twelve o'Clock, and close at Ten.

Vivat Rex.

N.B. The Booth is fitted up in a most commodious manner, for the better reception of Gentlemen, &c. &c.

———

"*Daily Advertiser*, April 26, 1742.

"At the Great Booth, Tottenham-Court, on Wednesday next, the 28th instant, will be a trial of manhood between the two following champions:

"Whereas I, WILLIAM WILLIS, commonly known by the name of the *fighting* Quaker, have fought Mr. SMALLWOOD about twelve months since, and held him the tightest to it, and bruised and battered him more than any one he ever encountered, though I had the ill-fortune to be beat by an accidental fall; the said SMALLWOOD, flushed with the success blind Fortune then gave him, and the weak attempts of a few vain Irishmen and boys, that have of late fought him for a minute or two, makes him think himself unconquerable; to convince him of the falsity of which, I invite him to fight me for ONE HUNDRED POUNDS, at the time and place above-mentioned, when, I doubt not but I shall prove the truth of what I have asserted, by pegs, darts, hard blows, falls, and cross-buttocks.

"WILLIAM WILLIS."

"I, THOMAS SMALLWOOD, known from my intrepid manhood and bravery on and off the stage, accept the challenge of this *puffing Quaker*, and will shew him that he is led by a false spirit, that means him no other good than that he should be chastised for offering to take upon him the *arm of the flesh*.

"THOMAS SMALLWOOD."

"*Note.* The doors will be opened at Ten, and the combatants mount at Twelve.

"There will be several by-battles, as usual; and particularly one between *John Divine* and *John Tipping*, for five Pounds each."

In this second trial of skill between Smallwood and Willis, the superiority of the former was again manifested, and the *fighting* Quaker retired with a *broken* spirit, and was *shown-up* as a complete *Ranter!* Smallwood beat him easy; notwithstanding his terrible threats of "pegs, darts, hard blows, and cross-buttocks."

The *calls of honour*, it appears, were numerous to be settled, and little time was suffered to intervene from the following public notice:

"May 24, 1742, at *George Taylor's* Booth, Tottenham-court-road,—There will be a trial of manhood to-morrow, between the following champions, viz.

"Whereas I, JOHN FRANCIS, commonly known by the name of the *Jumping Soldier*, who have always had the reputation of a good fellow, and have fought several bruisers in the street, &c. nor am I ashamed to mount the stage when my manhood is called in question by an Irish braggadocio, whom I fought some time ago, in a by-battle, for twelve minutes, and though I had not the success due to my courage and ability in the art of boxing, I now invite him to fight me for Two Guineas, at the time and place above-mentioned, where, I doubt not, I shall give him the truth of a good beating.

"JOHN FRANCIS."

"I PATRICK HENLEY, known to every one for the truth of a good fellow, who never refused any one on or off the stage, and fight as often for the diversion of gentlemen as money, do accept the challenge of this *Jumping Jack*; and shall, if he don't take care, give him one of my bothering blows, which will convince him of his ignorance in the art of boxing.

"PATRICK HENLEY."

Paddy kept his promise, for he so *bothered the gig* of the Jumping Soldier, that he was not able to *move*, much more to *jump*, for some time : Paddy gave him a Tipperary *fling*, which so completely *shook* all his recollection out of him, that he never troubled the town afterwards with any more of his *epistolary* challenges!

About this time it was hinted to Broughton by the *sporting world*, that a more eligible place was necessary than Taylor's Booth for their accommodation, and that if Broughton would undertake the management of such a house, a subscription would be entered into to defray the expences of the same by the nobility and gentry. Under the cognizance of so respectable a firm, a building was soon erected, denominated Broughton's New Amphitheatre, every way convenient and fit for the purpose, in what is now called *Hanway-street*, Oxford-street. In its interior appearance, it was somewhat similar to Astley's Riding-School, with boxes, pit, and gallery, and a commodious stage for the combatants, and which was opened on March 10, 1743, with the following public notice :—

AT BROUGHTON'S NEW AMPHITHEATRE,

OXFORD-ROAD,

The back of the late Mr. Fig's,

On Tuesday next, the 13th instant,

Will be exhibited

THE TRUE ART OF BOXING,

By the *eight famed* following men, viz.

ABRAHAM	EVANS,	———	ROGER,
———	SWEEP,	———	ALLEN,
———	BELAS,	ROBERT SPIKES, and	
———	GLOVER,	HARRY GRAY, the	
		Clog-maker.	

The above eight men are to be brought on the Stage, and to be matched according to the approbation of the gentlemen who shall be pleased to honour them with their company.

N. B.   There will be a *Battle Royal* between the

NOTED BUCKHORSE,

and *seven* or *eight* more; after which there will be several *By-battles* by others.

Gentlemen are therefore desired to come by times. The doors will be open at nine; the champions mount at eleven; and no person is to pay more than *a Shilling*.

If it should appear that the *mind* is debased from witnessing such public displays; if the *customs* and *manners* of society were infringed upon by such exhibitions; and if the feelings of men were so blunted from these specimens of hardihood and valour, as to prevent them from fulfilling those public situations in life, which many are called upon to perform with fidelity, justice, and reputation—then would Pugilism be a disgrace to that country where it is permitted, and boxers rendered obnoxious to society?

However, in point of argument and fact, it has perhaps become necessary to enquire, how far, in patronizing Pugilism, the effects of which manly art have operated upon those minds, so as to reduce their consequence in the estimation of their friends, or injure their public character with society in general, have taken place?

It is an incontrovertible fact, that one of the most celebrated and exalted civic characters in the nation, whose patriotic attention toward the preservation and due administration of the laws; whose firmness in supporting, upon all occasions, the liberty of the subject; whose dignity and consistency of conduct in representing the first city in the world in parliament; also in fulfilling one of the most important official situations, the Lord Mayor of London; that, upon his retiring from that most arduous and honourable situation—(a situation rendered difficult and of imminent peril, from the badness of the times and scarcity of provisions,) which he filled with so much humanity toward the consideration of the people, and so perfectly constitutional in its practice, adding stability to the civil power, and reflecting lustre upon the protection of the laws—it is upon record, no individual ever received more public thanks. His patriotic conduct was not only admired throughout England, but on being presented to the First Consul, Buonaparte, at Paris, his fame had so far ran before him, that he was complimented by that celebrated character in the following words, "that while the *civil power* was strong enough, never to call in the aid of the military!" It appears, then, that the name of Harvey Christian Coombe never suffered the slightest tarnish from his patronage of the Old English custom of Boxing in the early part of his life, but through a long and distinguished career pourtrayed such fortitude of disposition, and proved his pretensions so clear to the character of a real Englishman, an honest citizen, and an independent senator, that, in October 12, 1812, Alderman Coombe was placed at the head of the poll, by the voices of 5125 independent livery-men, creating a majority of 548 votes over the highest ministerial candidate. He was also returned the fourth time as member for the City of London, for his past services, and as a conspicuous and interesting ornament to the nation.

If the opinion of that senator be of any weight, whose speeches have been so often loudly cheered in the House of Commons, whose enlightened mind, classical acquirements, and transcendant talents have so delighted and refined the senses of his auditors by his brilliant wit—his figurative imagination, and irresistible eloquence—a mind stored with researches from ancient and modern literature, united with a conversant practice of the character and knowledge of mankind, in all its various gradations, from the *rusticity* of a cudgelling bout at a country fair—the humours of a *bull bait*—the *minutiæ* of a boxing match, down to the finished elegance of *Royalty*—he has thus publicly declared his sentiments;—

"A smart contest, this, between Maddox and Richmond! Why are we to boast so much of the *native* valour of our troops, as shewn at Talavera, at Vimeira, and at Maida, yet to discourage all the practices and habits which tend to keep alive the same sentiments and feelings? The sentiments that filled the minds of the three thousand spectators who attended the two Pugilists were just the same in kind as those which inspired the higher combatants on the occasion before enumerated.—It is the circumstances only in which they are displayed that make the difference.

"He that the world subdued, had been
But the best wrestler on the green."

There is no sense in the answer always made to this, '*Are no men brave but boxers?*' Bravery is found in all habits, classes, circumstances, and conditions. But have habits and institutions of one sort no tendency to form it more than of another?—Longevity is found in persons of habits the most opposite; but are not certain habits more favourable to it than others? The courage does not arise from mere boxing, from the mere beating or being beat: but from the sentiments excited by the contemplation and cultivation of such practices.

Will it make no difference in the mass of people, whether their amusements are all of a pacific, pleasurable, and effeminate nature; or whether they are of a sort that calls forth a continued admiration of prowess and hardihood?"

Then if such an enlightened senator as the late Right Hon. W. Windham felt no hesitation in promulgating the above sentiments respecting the utility of Pugilism as a *national trait*, there appears no necessity whatever, that any of its *professors* stand in need of an Apology!

> Strange is it, that our bloods,
> Whose colour, weight, and heat pour'd out together,
> Would quite confound distinction, yet stand off
> In difference mighty. But do not so—

Memoirs

OF

THE LIFE OF THOMAS CRIBB.

NOTHING but a thirst of power first made conquerors; the desire of quiet possession induced these men to exterminate the first possessors: both together rendered the agents employed in such aggrandisements, ferocious, and blood-thirsty. They carried into private life the same notions of brutal force, and the desire to annihilate opposition by death; nor was it until generations had passed away, that the inhabitants of countries so obtained, settled down into the peaceful habits of domestic or social life; for man is naturally gregarious, and the lover of his species.

The sports of the field, and the destruction of animals considered noxious, or those requisite for the table, constituted the sole enjoyment of our forefathers; but the introduction of foreign luxuries, and the consequent amassment of wealth and show, brought with them pride and contumely, that descended to the lowest paths of life. Qualities these which our proud spirits say *must be repressed*; for the bare exhibition of newly got riches, and thence the assumption of superiority, which, having no *personal* existence, is only to be found in those possessions, is an insult upon common sense.

Austere *looks* from old acquaintance, or neighbours newly elevated, and offensive *words*, not to call them opprobrious, begat the desire of retaliation; and the ready means being in every man's *hands*, a box on the *ear*, or in the *eye*, seems to point out the most appropriate mode of retaliating immediately upon the offended organs of sense. This appears to us the way in which *the row* began, which has since obtained the term *boxing*; a word derived from *a box*, which may be supposed to contain the rich moveables that caused the pride and offensive actions of the person so *boxed.* But in whatever way its origin may be argued and settled, no doubt exists of boxing, as an art, being entirely English; the English are confessedly, a proud and boisterous race, hard to control, impatient of restraint, lovers of liberty individually, but anxious to command and to control others. Hence the commanding aspect, the voice of authority, the love of law, the enormous increase of statutes, the admiration of prize-boxers and boxing, the despication of missiles, the absence of assassination, the prevalence of athletic exercises and manly sports; hence the generous mind that is trained to a true and dignified investigation of all those topics, and more—and hence the general desire for information thereon, which has led to the present series of Memoirs, and of which the actual champion necessarily takes the lead.

THOMAS CRIBB is a native of the parish of Bitton, in Gloucestershire, about five miles from Bristol, having been born at the village of Hanham, the 8th of July, 1781, so far as we can collect, the name not appearing in the parish register-book of that period. Situated in the same parish are Kingswood and Cockerwood, places much renowned for coals and boxing; and the subject of this Memoir, in common with all other of the commonality thereabout, was early initiated in both. Indeed most of our Bristolians of *fisty* note trace their origin to the district of these pits, or the neighbouring county of Somerset; a hardy race, living free and unrestrained, and imposing the task on all they deal with, of knowing how to take care of themselves in any disputes that may arise. The course of their trading lies in carrying coals into the adjoining towns, upon teams of horses, dispersing here and there to sell their commodity, and returning home at night; but, upon the least suggestion of unfairness, or intrusion, as regards the commerce in coals— fists, not law—thumps, not stilettos—settle the contests. They fight about the women sometimes, the same as *other people* do about love-affairs: boxing-matches also take place for small prizes, or because the parties may not like each other, "to zee which o'n's the best man;" a fight is nocked up at times for amusement, at others for exercise, or "just to ha' a bit of vun," as they term it. In the parish of Cowley, not far distant, we formerly knew of a tolerably respectable farmer, whose five sons were in the habit of fighting every time they returned from Bristol or Gloucester market, by way of adjusting the accounts of the day, and who, at his retiring from the farm, left it in these words:—"Ben can lather all vour of his brothers, zo let *he* ha't," and he had the farm accordingly, though the youngest son.

Though all the places above mentioned go under the comprehensive name of "the Kingswood collieries," yet the recesses of Cockerwood, where Cribb's relations lived, afforded a secure retreat to persons who might render themselves obnoxious to the law; so that lost horses, which might *stray* thither, seldom found their way back for a *season*, and the owners' friends were seldom numerous enough to *seek* after them. A circumstance that superinduced a good share of courage into the young coal-carriers, as well as their parents: but civilization and a better order of things have been long introduced there, to the great ease and comfort of the aged and well-disposed.

The spirit, however, remains; and when the increase of population, which is rapid, excites a desire, or imposes the necessity, of emigration *into* Bristol, *over* to Bath, or *up* to London, the same spirit is infused into the succeeding generation; and thus we have, from the first named city and emporium of the west, a greater number of well-crossed pugilists, who are chicken-taught, ever fighting, indomptable at odds, and always alert, scientific, quick hitters, and courageous. These prime qualities of the Bristol school are to be found, some two or three of them, at least, in every individual (though not always exercised) throughout the whole *district* that surrounds the city whose name it bears, and which we would call "the boxing district" but for two reasons. *First*, because we are averse to the coining of new or unheard-of names; and, *secondly*, because towards the southern part of it, a good deal of *single-stick* and *wrestling* are introduced along with fisty-cuffs; so that we sometimes notice at *wakes* or *revels* (as they are termed "down along,") the same sports shall be composed of all three kinds of forceful exertion for the mastery on the same day; nay, we have seen the same men enter the ring to "cudgel," who afterwards undertook to carry off the prize at wrestling, and who finished each of those trials of skill with a few rounds at boxing. However, this district extends on that side some twenty miles towards Gloucester (exclusively;) thence westward to the sea are included the manufacturing places, Dursley, Uly, Wotton, and Stroudwater, where they all fight, there being in the latter place, on the navigation, some tremendous hammermen. Eastwards, it extends to Chippenham only.

Towards Bath, the district for native boxers may be said to extend the whole way, exclusive of its own polite jurisdiction; thence its course is well marked, partly into Wiltshire; and westward, in a zigzag, undulating manner, to the bottom of Somersetshire. Less distinctly we might say, its seeds and germinating property appear here and there, throughout the remainder of the *four counties*, Dorset, Devon, and Cornwall, in which latter they usually turn out "one and all;" whilst in the preceding county they fight from earliest childhood for a bellyful, or for fun, and occasionally turn out a very good man or two.

We thought this brief account of the means whereby the heroes of the Bristol-school acquire the expert use of their fists in early life, an appropriate introduction to memoirs of the life of the present chief of that school, although not the most expert among them; reserving more particulars to a subsequent part of our labours, where we shall treat on Boxing considered as a Science, its first principles, and modes of conducting the contest to a safe conclusion; in all which points we have no hesitation in saying thus early—the Bristol or Belcherian school excels all others.

Tom Cribb arrived in London in 1795, being then at the tender age of thirteen years old, though a stout youth. He was directed to a relative of his mother, a bell-hanger by trade, with whom having dodged about some time, he at length *plied* at the coal-wharfs along Wapping! a profitable and appropri-

ate employment for young fellows who have great strength, and are of tolerably sober habits, both of which he possessed in no common degree. The *turn-ups* inseparable from the profession, brought Cribb into notice throughout that neighbourhood, where he received for cognomen—*"The black Diamond,"* as being expressive of his calling and his pluck. This however, is now known to depend so much upon constitutional strength, or the actual state of body at the time of contestation, that severe training is found to answer every purpose of bracing the system, and restoring it to that desirable state; and when conducted with due skill and perseverance, renders the subject thereof less vulnerable to external injuries. Cribb, on the contrary, possessed the best of constitutions naturally, as was evinced upon occasion of his being capsized from one of those boards that lead from barge to barge, and on which the workmen traverse each other with much peril, considering the rise and fall of the tide, which constantly affects the position of the barges, and, consequently, the security of those boards. Over one of these, between the craft, he fell with his load, and got jammed in a dreadful manner, but recovered, after awhile, by dint of a good stamina, and, it seems, took to miscellaneous employment, though equally honourable to that of coal porter; for we find him, not long after, subjected to another accident that occasioned a troublesome spitting of blood. Having a double chest of oranges on his head, his heels slipped up, and the chest alighted on his breast, an accident which would have cost an ordinary man his life, as we have witnessed. Hereupon he went to sea, and though we hear no reports of this interesting period of his life, no doubt he did his duty manfully.

We choose to state these particulars, because it frequently happens that men are good men, though they may not yet have entered the ring; and this latter piece of information more particularly, because that man is a dastard who, at some period or other of his life, has not *found* an opportunity of serving against the enemy; especially when the demand is urgent and the public peril great.

At the conclusion of the *short peace*, he got discharged (1803); and towards the close of the next year, having exhibited himself no little, he was pitched upon to fight the veteran George Maddox. The meeting took place on Wood Green, two miles north of Highgate, on Monday, 7th of January, 1805. Maddox, though then nearly fifty years of age, and two inches shorter than Cribb, who was then scarcely twenty-four, possessed so much bottom and science that, at setting-to, the odds were very little against him: he too came from a fighting ancestry, and on one occasion had been seconded by his sister. On this occasion, however, Paddington Jones seconded him, while *Black Sam* very sympathetically seconded our *Black Diamond*.

Whoever persuaded Cribb to prefer an old good one for his trial-battle (or *debut* in the ring) was in the right; but he should also have guarded him against the ill-usage to which *young* pugilists, without powerful support, are too commonly subjected, when they seem in a fair way of winning the battle. For many men lay wagers (or bet) with a determination "not to lose" upon any suit; so if the subject (no matter what,) goes against them, they endeavour to joke off the whole affair; if that wont do, they quarrel it off; if this again will not do, they then fight it off—so they have three chances to one against honourable persons. But as for Cribb himself, he can look back upon this early part of his milling career, without finding much cause of complaint when 'tis put in the balance with some of his subsequent contests, when he in turn was the favourite of those who endeavour *not to lose* at any rate. He himself, however, is not to be charged with any participation in the scene that took place in one of his subsequent battles, when the ring was broke to prevent his defeat. Neither is he quarrelsome in his cups, beyond a proneness to laying wagers and to press them stiffly; on the contrary, he appeals to the law and magistracy rather too hastily for our notions; a larrup in the head being a more appropriate punishment for some kinds of insults, and an amicable reference of legal disputes better than 'going to a jury.'

His second battle was fought with Tom *Tough* (Blake by name,) on Blackheath, for a purse of forty guineas. The money had been collected by subscription on the day of his last fight, and took place the 15th of Feb. following. Cribb's arm was too long for the science of Blake, and for the first quarter of an hour, the latter could make no impression upon Cribb, but absolutely broke down his prowess by baffling it with superior strength. While Blake was manœuvring in breathless anxiety to go in, Cribb kept an arm extended, over which he fought, retreating; until his antagonist committing some fault, or becoming exhausted, he had an opportunity to place some hits worth remembering; and it is worthy remark here, that Cribb never made his blows *tell* so well, nor acted offensively to so much effect, as when Blake exerted himself the most. Altogether, we were forcibly reminded of this contest three years afterwards, when Horton proceeded in the same manner with Cribb, that Blake did upon the present occasion; both of them dancing round with more of *spar* than of *fight* in him, and when they had spirit to venture upon going-in, each caught '*toco for yam.*' The conqueror was punished about the head in this second contest, which did not happen so materially in the subsequent one, to which we now allude; indeed, all his battles may be said to have been described in this single one, with one or two such exceptions as this now made.

So much satisfaction did the gentlemen amateurs feel at the prowess of our hero, that no time was lost in again matching him; and he fought Ikey Pig, on the 21st of May, 1805, for another forty guineas, raised as before, and again conquered his man. This was a Jew of remarkably athletic form, about the shoulders especially, with sledge-hammer fists; Cribb was the favourite with the subscribers, but Ikey with the Israelites, and the latter wanted odds at first, but gave them in the early part of the contest, inasmuch as Cribb was floored several times. This, however, was the *legal* means of causing the opponent to exhaust his superior strength; which end it effected, hit and drop being equal to hit and get away, particularly if that plan bothers the adversary, and is the common finesse of the native Bristol school of pugilism. What was more surprising, Mr. Ikey Pig (or Pic) sung out "enough" at the end of the 11th round, while Cribb was yet down on the ground, whither one of the Jew's blows seems to have sent him! The

thing "was strange, 'twas passing strange, 'twas wonderful."
—N. B. At each fall, and there were no less than seven, you
might perceive Tom feeling for his opponent's ribs—two or
three of his blows being very successfully placed.

Upon the termination of this contest, the betters upon Ikey
chaffed a good deal about "falling down," and though another
Jew (Josephs) made a specific agreement on that point *with
his antagonist*, yet it went for nothing; (or all my eye, Betty
Martin,) for the words "without a blow," being introduced,
brought back the affair to its original standard.

Paddington Jones, who seconded Cribb at this fight, took
umbrage at something or other, and joining with the adverse
party, afterwards carried over the plans and tactics of his former friend to the *enemy*. Jones was alway a good, active, and
intelligent second, and took in, at a glance, the means adopted
by his principal, to secure the victory; accordingly, he not
only seemed very forward in promoting the next battle in
which Cribb was engaged; but he seconded the opposing man,
so effectually, that he procured the defeat of his former friend;
thus adding one more illustration of our practical remarks regarding *good seconding-men*, in another page of this Number.
One Dick Hall, who was no great shakes, either way, picked
up Cribb upon this occasion, and proved himself but an ordinary man for the situation.

George Nicholls, a butcher, from the neighbourhood of
Bristol, having been previously *tried-on* by Jones, was now
brought by him to tackle Cribb, for a purse of £25, at Black-
water. He proved himself a good fellow, smiled during the
earlier part of the battle, and fought much in Cribb's once
cautious manner, with the left arm much extended. It was
tedious work to behold, until the men were pricked a little;
though Nicholls was the gayest man of the two, and saw well
the moment for planting a blow in the *first* round. Nicholls
imparted the first clean knock-down blow; in the *fourth* Cribb
stopped George's forwardness by a left-handed facer. Several
good rallies took place, to the nineteenth round, when one of
Cribb's peepers seemed *dark*, and from that time, to the end
of the fortieth round, he seldom had any advantage, and grad-

ually lost ground. However, he stood up to be hit at for twelve more rounds, when he gave in.*

Bill Richmond† pretended to fight Cribb, for a match of 25 guineas, the 8th of October, 1805, at Hailsham, in Sussex, but it proved "all my eye:" the black hopped and danced round his man, and protracted the contest for an hour and a half, and then cried 'enough' with a smile, but without making a mark upon the steady nob of our hero. The Duke of Clarence, who was present, appeared to enjoy the frolic of blackey; to us, however, it was mere burlesque, and ought not to have been tolerated one minute.

Eighteen months passed away before Cribb was again called upon to contest the palm of victory; when his patron, Captain Barclay, matched him against Jem Belcher, for 200 guineas. Jem, it will be recollected, lost an eye by a racket-ball, but still retaining the title of Champion, he must necessarily undertake any man that might offer or resign the honour.‡ They met accordingly the 8th of April, 1807, at Moulsey-hurst, Belcher being the favourite 3 to 2, and moreover, on entering the ring, he betted Cribb 25 guineas to 20 on the event. But our hero was in the primest state of health, was

---

*That false notion of being serviceable to a man by suppressing some adverse fact concerning him, was long practised regarding this defeat of Cribb, all mention whereof was omitted in the publications of the day; whilst he who had been primarily guilty of this unmanly suppression, stood convicted before the public, yet he set up a loud complaint at the inutility of such a mode of proceeding.

† He, and the other blacks, are usually termed 'men of *colour*,' by the scribes of pugilism; but, alas, poor souls! let them be told, a black man is not a man of colour, nor is the man of colour black, in any of the countries where both are to be found: this is some of the erroneous cant of the ring, introduced by —— ——, and followed every where by sensual ignorance.

‡ Our determination to do justice superinduces one or two observations. The incomparable man who was now doomed to resign his honours, besides the loss of an eye, had been much reduced in strength by disease and irregularity; the latter might be restored, partly, by a mode of training adapted to such circumstances, but what power could restore to him an eye, that valuable member so necessary to the proper planting of his blows? As one way of providing the remedy, We ourselves undertook to press on the consideration of Belcher and his friend, the propriety of stipulating that Cribb should in fairness, at each set-to, have an adhesive plaister placed over his eye, leaving to chance its being knocked off the next moment. This proposition, however, went no farther, Jem continuing to think he could easily close up at least one eye of his antagonist; and John Gully coinciding in the same opinion, the matter dropped where it originated, at the Plough, in Carey-street.

known to be a glutton, and on this occasion turned out to be a better sparrer than hitherto; whereas Jem required a greater length of time, and different training to what he did receive, besides being "down in the mouth," at having lost, by death, his old and fast friend, Mr. Fletcher Reid.

Belcher could not, and in effect did not, last long enough to service his opponent to the truth, though up to the fifteenth round the bets rose so high as 4 to 1 in his favor. In the eighteenth round Belcher sprained his wrist, and having received a hit over his perfect eye, as might be anticipated, he threw away his blows and exhausted his power upon the superior strength of his adversary. Forty-one rounds—in thirty-five minutes, transferred the Championship from Belcher to Cribb; but scarcely a man of sensibility in the ring failed to lament the thing as pitiable; and nothing but the uniform moderation and steady uprightness of the present Champion can reconcile them to it: Jem Belcher was never beat: it was only a *part* of him that was beat. So much was this the public opinion, that although Cribb had so obtained the Championship *de facto*, he was not hailed as such, *de jure*, until the period of his first fight with Molineux.

Thirteen months spell brought Cribb in contact with Horton, who had conquered George Cribb, at Bristol; but this latter is a swell cur—and—and was beat. Tom, however, met him on Wednesday, the 1st of May, 1808, in the same ring that Gully afterwards contested with Gregson, the match being for 100 guineas (10 forfeit); Horton's system of hitting was so much unlike any thing we have witnessed, excepting that his fiddlesticks seemed always at play to little tune, that he only came within reach of Cribb to be marked: "Go home to thy mother," said Tom, "she won't knaw thee agen." About half an hour extinguished this pupil of *the chicken*, as a boxer; though betting was even to the moment of setting-to, when Barclay offered 5 to 4, 6 to 4, and 7 to 4, successively, on Cribb, which some few accepted of.

Next Gregson, who had been twice vanquished by John Gully, undertook Tom Cribb, but this circumstance, combined with those we have related, immediately raised the odds a shade or two in favour of Cribb, and at setting-to there were no takers at 5 to 4. This was confessedly the most interesting fight the Champion had yet engaged in: the equal *degree* of science, (though of two sorts), the consonance in the degree of activity also possessed by them, and the knowledge that the term *Champion* would be conferred on the conqueror—since Gully had retired, altogether conspired to excite the public interest in no common manner. It took place at Moulseyhurst, the 25th of October, 1808. Paul Methuen, Esq. backed Cribb for 300 guineas, whilst Gregson had for patron the Marquis of Twedale; and besides those there were on the ground the Duke of York, Lords Craven, Somerville, Barrymore, Brook, and Yarmouth, and good numbers of the young nobility and gentry.

Neither were men ever better attended *within the ropes* (thirty feet) than on this occasion, and, at half-past twelve, Cribb and Gregson entered at opposite points; the first man followed by Gully and Bill Gibbons, Gregson by Jem Belcher and Richmond. The *first* round, both hit ineffectually; in the *second*, Cribb avoided three well-meant blows of his adversary, planted two body blows and a cutting facer, whence flowed first blood, and in a mutual rally threw his man. No *harm* done yet. In the *third* round, Gregson, quite alive, flew at Cribb and put in a blow under the ear, that Tom did not completely recover from through the fight;* he stepped back, Gregson following with too little caution, and at every move poor Bob's head stopped just as many blows as he advanced paces—say seven or eight. Science he had none, but stupefaction plenty: all those blows were good, neither amounting to a knock down, but all told, and affected him to the centre, when he sunk.

In the *fourth*, Cribb stood in need of breathing time, and he fell in making play—*a-la-mode de Bristole*. The *next* round, his second having put him up to it, Gregson sparred for the first hit, which he obtained—the best we ever saw him put in, upon the temple of Tom, who in turn seemed stupified and all abroad,

---

* Here Gregson ought to have *sparred* in search of another such a blow, as the adversary must have come to receive it.

and thereupon in a rally he was knocked off his legs. [Here Bob was wrong again: he now ought to have milled away jollily, hit him in *the mark*, and indeed done as he liked with him.] In the following round, Gregson resumed his wonted impetuosity, and suffered in consequence, every time to the *thirteenth* round, when he showed signs of weakness, while Cribb gained second wind and fresh spirits, though not distinguishable upon the muscles of his face—they were so disfigured. Gregson's in the same state, his mouth sadly cut. Up to the twenty-second round the same series of milling continued, Cribb punching away, and Gregson once knocking his man down, and at the last giving him the Lancashire purr with so much effect, that Tom fell as if to rise no more; and the feeling that he could not come again induced bets to that effect, 10 to 1—"Done;" but bottom does it after science is forgotten, and he appeared at the scratch for the twenty-third time. Hit they could not, any more than babies; so they struggled like old women, Gregson was thrown, and, when time was called, could not *come again*; but the words were scarcely pronounced when Cribb fell as if he had swooned away.

Pluck, however, and a sense of mental injuries received from Richmond, during the contest, incited him to offer the black a set-to at once for £50; that which characterises the Bristol *boys* to a hair (double battles being usual), but could not be allowed. Throughout the affair Richmond had been playing his monkey tricks, making wry-mouths at Tom, and chirruping a good deal at every vicissitude that befel him; a mode of conduct we have all along discouraged, which it is now hoped has arrived at its termination, or else punishment must take place on the spot, notwithstanding the confusion that must ensue.

Mr. Methuen presented Cribb with £150 for his gallant behaviour.

————o☉o————

FEMALE PUGILISM.—On the morning of Tuesday last, a great concourse of people were attracted toward a spot called the "Ruins," near St. George's Fields, to witness the prowess of two *Ladies* residing in Kent-street, who appeared (attended by two *other Ladies* as seconds) in short jackets, secured at the waist by a handkerchief, their hair cropt expressly for the present pur-

pose, and all *in prime twig*, determined on a *regular mill*. By what we could collect, *Sal* had been flirting with *Nan's* favoured lover; which unpardonable offence, *her own constancy* and *affection* could but ill brook. The *Ladies* on coming up to the *scratch*, displayed *fine science*, but were *cautious*. *Nan made play*, but *Sal* was not *to be had*, and fought rather *shy*. Some manœuvring ensued, when *Nan*, making a *feint*, *Sal* attempted to put in a left-handed hit, which was well stopped by the former, who placed a blow near the place where *Sally* took her snuff, and which made her *ivories* dance a reel in their box.

Round 2. *Nancy* received a *stomager* which made her *smile* for two minutes; but she paid back the compliment with *interest*, and placed a well-meant *favour* upon *Sally's* right *ogle*; 5 to 4 on *Nancy*.

3. This was a good manly—(we beg our readers pardon, but we had really forgotten that we were speaking of the *softer* sex) a good *womanly* round; some tremendous blows were given and exchanged, but *Sally's* foot slipping, *Nancy made the best possible use of time*, and planting a heavy hit *a la Randall*, *Sally* was *floored*, and the *claret* flowed prodigiously from her upper lip— 6 to 2, on *Nancy*.

4, 5, and 6. *Sally* unexpectedly sprang from the arms of the *Lady* who seconded her, whilst *Nancy* was exulting in the equity of her cause and her partial success:—she was taken rather off her guard, a close followed, and both went down, *Nancy* undermost, but they scrambled up without aid, and a sort of *pully-hauley* business ensued.

7. Both appeared to be out of breath, their heads smoking like a Glass House—*Sally* seemed distressed, whilst her antagonist played off in the *weaving* system in *prime style*, and following up her success, completely spoiled the look of her adversaries *mug*, as she *tipt* her a *cross-buttock*; throwing her head *into chancery* and her body into the dirt at the same time.—6 to 4 on *Nancy*.

8, 9, 10. These rounds were more like a pull-cap concern for a *sweet-heart* between two nursery-maids, than an exhibition of *science* between *Ladies* possessing *their* abilities;—but we must, in justice, acknowledge they were *both* already beaten.

The 11th round would have created a belief in a spectator who had seen that round *only*, that it was "all a joke;" they hugged each other round the neck, and had they not been *cropt*, it is a matter of doubt if they would not have resorted to *pulling hair*—not to say *clawing faces*. Fortunately in this *rencontre* there was no *time* kept; or each in turn must have been *counted out*.— The seconds (or *Ladies in Waiting*) proposed a glass of *strip-me-naked*, which was mutually agreed to; and a delay of *business* ensued for the space of 20 minutes. *Sally* then changed her plan of attack. *Nancy* appeared *awake*, and breaking her guard, ran in to her like a bull-dog,—a well-contested rally followed, in which, however, *Sally* received a *floorer*, and lay for about three minutes regardless of all the cares of this world. This round decided the battle, although, after *Sally* had been refreshed with another glass of *strip-me-naked*, (of which *Nancy* also partook,) she proved herself *thorough bottom*, and stood 6 or 8 *baby-play* rounds afterwards, and even then swore—*said*, we mean, that "*she'd die afore she'd give in.*" She was, indeed, a perfect *glutton*; and *Nancy's* nobleness of soul was equally great and conspicuous, who "*declared as how she scorned to take adwantage not ower nobody at all.—Sal was all-vays thorough game,* and she didn't like her not none the *vusser faw* it."

The seconds complimented them both upon their magnanimity of conduct, and, apparently well pleased with themselves, and with each other, they all retired to *Daffy's* to sign a treaty of peace over another *kevarton* of *Blue Ruin.*

ANECDOTES AND RECOLLECTIONS OF DEPARTED PUGILISTS.

As it is professedly the intention of the conductors of the FANCY not to continue the Memoirs of Pugilists from number to number, thereby keeping the reader in suspence for the connecting parts, but rather to give a summary of their characters and prowess at one view; we shall hereafter devote a small part of our pages occasionally to anecdotes and recollections of those who are no longer *figurantes* on the *great stage* of this world.

DAN DONNELLY.—It is stated of the late Champion of Ireland, that on the day previous to his encounter with Oliver, a certain noble Lord called upon DONNELLY at Riddlesdown, about the middle of the day, and in the course of conversation, remarked rather tauntingly, "*that he might expect to have a pretty head and face from the effects of Oliver's fist, about the same time to-morrow.* DONNELLY, who was by no means a dry subject, looking his Lordship full in the face, replied with much jocularity and ironical expression, "*That he was not born in a wood to be scared by an owl.*" The smartness of the reply produced a hearty laugh against the amateur of rank; who by way of *softening* the matter, betted Donnelly £15 to 10 upon Oliver, which the *Irish Champion* immediately accepted.

It is also highly worthy of being recorded to the honor of the Irish Champion, that when he entered the apartment of the defeated Oliver after the battle, the coloured handkerchief which he had won belonging to his fallen opponent, he would not publicly wear as a trophy of victory, or to wound the feelings of *Oliver,* but took care to conceal it by way of a pad in the green handkerchief which he wore round his neck.

Many poetical effusions issued from the Irish press at the death of Sir Daniel Donnelly, from which we select the following:—

DIRGE OVER SIR DANIEL DONNELLY.
TUNE.—"*Molly Ashlore.*"

As down Exchequer-street* I strayed, a little time ago,
I chanced to meet an honest blade, his face brimful of woe;
I ask'd him why he seem'd so sad, or why he sigh'd so sore,
O Gramachree, Och, Tom, says he, Sir Daniel is no more.

---

* In Dublin.

With that he took me straight away, and pensively we went,
To where poor Daniel's body lay, in wooden waistcoat pent;
And many a yard before we reached the threshold of his door,
We heard the keeners as they screeched, Sir Daniel is no more!

We entered soft, for feelings sad were stiring in our breast,
To take our farewell of the lad who now was gone to rest;
We took a drop of Dan's potheen,* and joined the piteous roar,
O, where shall be his fellow seen, since Daniel is no more!

His was the fist whose weighty dint, did Oliver defeat,
His was the fist that gave the hint, it need not oft repeat,
His was the fist that overthrew his rivals o'er and o'er,
But now we cry in Pillalu, Sir Daniel is no more!

Cribb, Cooper, Carter, need not fear great Donnelly's renown,
For at his *wake* we're seated here, while he is lying down;
For death, that primest swell of all, has laid him on the floor,
And left us here, alas! to bawl, Sir Daniel is no more!

EPITAPH.

Here lies Sir Daniel Donnelly, a pugilist of fame;
In Ireland bred and born was he, and he was genuine game;
Then if an Irishman you be, when you have read this o'er,
Go home and drink the memory, of him who is no more.

———

PEDESTRIANISM.—On Wednesday, 20th of March, Mr. Rathby, a gentleman of fortune, residing at the West end of the town, started to run 10 miles in 56 minutes, for a stake of 200 sovereigns. The match was made at a well known house in Bond Street, a fortnight ago, since which Mr. Rathby has been training. Time was the favorite at odds of 6 and 7 to 4. The spot of ground chosen was 2 miles on the Edgeware-Road. The pedestrian started at 7 o'clock, performing the distance in the following manner.

	miles.	min.	sec.
1	2	11	6
2	2	10	40
3	2	11	0
4	2	11	4
5	2	12	0
	—	—	—
	10	55	50

* Dan Donnelly kept a public house.

It will thus be seen that Mr. R. won by only 10 seconds, and being rather a heavy man he was much distressed. It is considered a first-rate performance, and considerable sums of money have changed hands upon the occasion.

Walking against Eating.—This sporting event was decided at a public-house at Knightsbridge: one Boyne, a labouring gardener, undertook for the trifling sum of half a crown to eat, without drinking, 24 red herrings, and two ounces of mustard, while the landlord, a corpulent man, walked half a mile on the road. The pedestrian performed his march in some what less than nine minutes: but the hero of the jaw-bone had in less than eight minutes completed his task, and waited the arrival of his opponent with a full pot, the first fruits of his victory.

Memoirs

OF

THE LIFE OF THOMAS HICKMAN,

BETTER KNOWN AS "THE GAS-LIGHT MAN."

WHAT we before remarked respecting the breed, or early initiation of men to the art of boxing, as applied to the Bristolians, holds good also, in a remarkable manner, to the aspiring young man whose real name, and fighting cognomen, appear at the head of this page. He undertook the defence of himself at a very tender age, and he relates with glee of his soon converting his dexterity and pluck into the means of offence to all the boys who exhibited any *notion of the thing* in the neighbourhood of his native place, whom he lathered in succession. This is precisely the sort of education adapted to form the best fighting *men*, early habits serving us, in every case and at every emergency;* and if to such early manifest advantages they add those of having overcome sturdy opposition, and of outwitting artful contrivances for obtaining those juvenile victories, they thereby fashion a plan or *school* of themselves, in which may be discovered each individual's characteristic mode of fighting; and which partakes invariably of the method pursued by those he has contended with, or observed approvingly while fighting. Thus we have the Bristol method, the Broughtonian method, the Hebrew method, the Staffordshire, and the Lancashire methods, or *no method*. Each

---

* John Kemble studied "Hamlet" when a boy, and often turned out of bed in the middle of the night to enact this his favourite part: and a celebrated musical composer had the best of us during *a month at Bath* formerly, by jumping up naked at all hours, to scrape upon his cremona some new narcotic crotchet which had entered his head while dozing.

man invariably adopts the peculiarities in any of those *methods*, or manners of fighting (we hesitate to call either "a system,") that may seem, or be found, by him best adapted to his own particular powers, and notions of the fit moment of attack, and the right point to be hit at. That of Tom Hickman is a small modification of the practice in those two *counties*, Birmingham being considered out of the district; and as more ferocious than scientific. Although he stands well up to his man, and bores away at him even before he gets warm, yet it cannot be denied, that he is then watching an opportunity for doing execution, and his favourite hit is on the jaw-bone. With the gloves he lately hit Shelton on the same spot so hard as to raise some doubts in the latter "whether his head was on his shoulders or not." Unlike Scroggins he seems desirous of making his blows *tell* upon the head or trunk, and unlike the *mere sparrers* he defends himself not at all; so that he comes between the two extremes, and might be said to have a mode of his own, unless he has in view the practice of that system of fighting we might term "the Hebrew school," from its having been introduced by Daniel Mendoza, and consists in catching the moment that any point presents itself unguarded, and momentarily throwing away the whole body upon that effort. But still he neither copies, nor is it in his *nature* to fall in with, the *pit-pat* hits from the shoulder, or rather the elbow, that characterises the Hebrew mode of sparring, and does admirably well for *show* but nothing else; for, in letting go the blow which finished Cooper, as noticed before, we observed his right leg quitted the ground at the moment the blow told, and Jack Scroggins remarked the same aloud; besides all which nothing on earth is more certain than the ruin of Thomas Hickman as a pugilist, from the moment he should be persuaded to learn the Hebrew mode of *acting* in this particular. Indeed, *sparring* of any sort does not belong to the man of whom we are about relating some particulars of his life, with an eye more especially to his combats since his entering *the ring*.

From a boy he continued to fight away all opponents, when he was discovered milling a man in the Borough, in such gallant style as 'twas a pleasure to behold. Tom Shelton gave

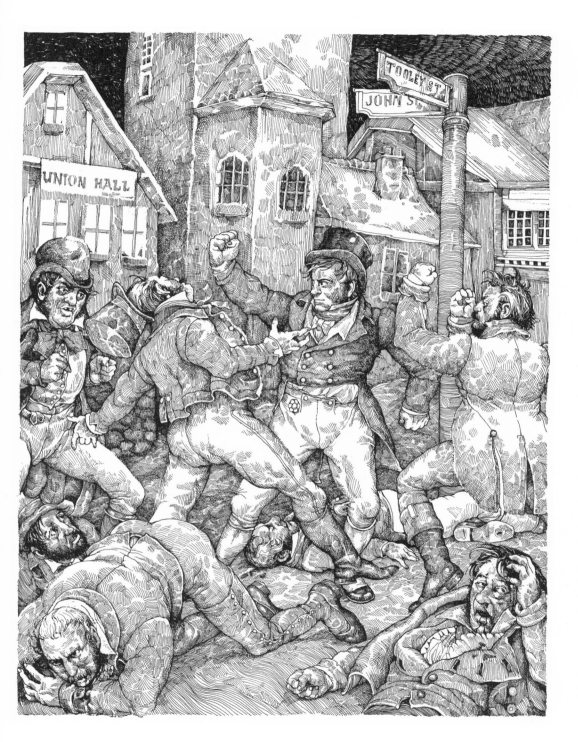

him an interview, and heard with satisfaction Hickman's re-
cital of his various feats; and they were found not fables but
facts; the first being with a youth called *Sedgeley*, at *Wedgbury
Cocking*; the second at same place, for a guinea a-side, with
Jock Miller; next a provincial conqueror named Hollis, for
five pounds a-side, both being strong men, while Tom was
still but a youth of seventeen, and causing him a good deal of
trouble. His fame was now up, and none offered their fists till
Lewky Walker, a man of weight and metal from the coal-pits,
raised the *two bits of rag* to put down against the like sum from
Hickman; however, master Luke had like to have been sacrificed in nineteen minutes time, which was all the receipt he
had for his money.

After his arrival in the metropolis, several turn-ups grace
the career of Thomas Hickman, in the intervals of as many
regular bouts for small sums, among which may be reckoned
two or three travelling sprees, up and down the streets, "when
insolence takes the wall of modest diffidence." We noticed
before, the circumstance of *seven* men lodging a complaint
against Hickman, at Union Hall, concerning his having milled
six of their body in John-street, Tooley-street. They were
mill-wrights by trade, who having taken umbrage at his behaviour, way-laid him and "caught a Tartar;" the magistrate
astonished at their story, and comparing the *size* of each of the
plaintiffs with that of the accused man, dismissed them with
rebukes at its improbability. He had, it seems, previously
given several men of their factory a taste of his prowess, and
in the gas-works where he was employed, took care to ap-
pease the turbulence of his own uproarious mates: this gave
rise to the 'foresaid conspiracy; but he "dissolved the con-
gress," as Dr. Slop might say.

Of the first-rate Gravel-lane men, he took the conceit out
of all who showed fight, and of some who barely showed their
noses:—1st. Bill Doughty, a smith, in thirteen minutes;—
2dly. Allix, a stupendous Irishman, who serviced Hickman,
and tossed him down oft and repeatedly, until the twentieth
round, when Tom having the best of him, planted a blow on
his whisker———— and "that is all about it," as the Deal-men

have it; so the reader may imagine the rest. *Thirdly*, he served
Jack Thomas nearly in the same style, and *fourthly* bouncing
Jack Andrews he *ditto-ed*, easily, though both decent ones.

Through the interest of Shelton, Hickman was matched to
undertake young Crawley for fifty pounds a-side, on Tuesday,
March the 16th, 1819, when he was 24 years of age, having
been born the 28th January, 1795. Crawley, though a tolerable sparrer, having some pluck, and a good deal of experience,
had enough of it in thirteen minutes. These considerations
gave much celebrity to 'the man of gas,' as he was termed, in
a poor pun upon the country of *Goliath* of old; and he was
matched to fight G. Cooper just a year afterwards. Cooper's
science of defence is undoubtedly great, his mode of hitting
elegant, but it was destined to be defeated by the unfinished
tactics of a "bang-up local;" and 'tis worth while to stop and
remark, that 7 to 4 was the current betting against Gas, notwithstanding *his accounts* of his prowess, which were to be
authenticated easily, and Shelton's proofs that he had fought
the principal part of his last battle with a broken finger. In
fourteen minutes and a half, however, Cooper could not come
again: though this event might have been anticipated from
the first round; in which Gas having hit a little short of his
mark (the whisker,) his fist came in contact with the tip of
his antagonist's nose, and driving the cartilage by a side twist
so as to dislocate the integuments a good way round, occasioned a great internal extravasation of blood. Cooper's countenance changed considerably in the next round; but recovered
a little upon the blood making its way to the mouth and throat,
where it burst forth, and nearly choked the man. Such are
among the effects of one of Tom Hickman's hits, as exemplified
in this his first fight with Cooper, which took place near Stowe
in Buckinghamshire, the 28th March, 1820; a kind of hit on
which we took occasion to descant at some length in our account of the second fight with the same man.

————o◯o————

Pugilistic Challenge. . . . The renowned *George Cooper* has intimated to the
gentlemen of the Scottish and Cumberland Fancy, that before he retires from
the prize ring, he is desirous of giving *Thomas Hickman*, the "Gas Man," a

touch of genuine science at Carlisle Races, the 29th of September next. Hickman's gasconade and vaunting in London is not to intimidate the hero of the northern metropolis; *George Cooper*, therefore, proposes to fight *Thomas Hickman*, at the time and place above-mentioned, for 200 guineas, in a forty feet ring, to be a fair stand-up fight, half minute time; or for 100 guineas in a twenty-four feet ring on the same terms. The umpires to have a discretionary power to give to the losing man, out of the stakes, such a sum as they may deem proper, by way of remuneration for his travelling and training expences; provided the sum to be given is agreed on before the commencement of the battle. *George Cooper* having already travelled upwards of a thousand miles to fight *Hickman*, for the gratification of the London Fancy, thinks he is privileged to demand a meeting at "merry Carlisle."

THE BATTLE

Between GEORGE COOPER, (*the Bargeman,*) *and* THOMAS HICKMAN
(*the Gas-Light Man,*) *for 100 Guineas a side.*

Much anxiety prevailed, as it always does when the fight is at a great distance, upon the word being given out, that the meeting would take place *at least thirty* miles from town; an anxiety that is mostly observable in those whose prads look most unlike lasters *down* and *up*. However Harpendon Common, three miles beyond St. Albans, having been fixed upon, the evening of Monday the 9th, and the plebian cattle that were to do work put into condition, by an extra handful of hay each, next morning saw these, with many a pedestrian, set out with their faces up Highgate-hill, followed here and there by a poney, or a cart of doubtful strength. These are the people who, being either idlers at home, or having arduous work to perform *round the ring*, 'take time by the forelock,' and hedge it down the evening before the fight, in order to get fresh upon *the ground*. The day was fine, and St. Albans filled with lodgers presented the spectacle of a town infested with fair folks, or "very like the evening before the races," as our hostess at the Pea-hen observed, with an *interesting* smile: *good beds* were here five shillings each, and other things in proportion. In short the whole business of the day was a *treat* to the people on that line of road, as well publicans as private ones; for as low down as *Platters*, the ladies who "split straws," (they are so nice about things,) every body was in motion. At returning, even Harry Harmer doff'd his benjamin, and kick'd up a reel at a road-side house, while the prads were baiting; and graver cits than he saw clearly enough at an early hour how this part of the business of the day would end. Cy. Davis brought home the intelligence at a quarter before four o'clock; having waited at Barnet with his horse ready saddled, and receiving a messenger there, he posted to town at that early hour; his was the first arrival in *the city*, though a wager had been laid at the Trumpeters on that point, and he rode up to the Castle tavern with the sad news, too soon for the pigeons in that quarter.

The *ring*, as agreed upon, was formed twenty-four feet *square*. This term, however, being a solecism, deserves notice here, since *a ring* cannot be *square*; but such is the slip-slop slangery of the day, for the company on foot do, at a distance, form a sort of circle approaching the rhomboidal shape. This, we maintain, is the only *ring* (giving that title to the persons who are admitted withinside it:) unless an outer circle, formed of vehicles of every description, and some non-descripts, may be termed another. Here, then, is the solution of the question, "what is the ring?" And although a *good one*, and true too, may be pounded never to have occurred to the sconce of any one person who ever entered the outer circle, from Mr. Jackson down to Johnny Raw, nor from the Stakeholder himself down to Pickpockets plenty." —— *A-propos des Bottes*,"* as Mr. — — would say. The pick-pockets were as audacious as usual, roving about in pretty lots of ten or fifteen each, and openly hustling and robbing whoever came in their way. Short as was the battle, several watches and purses were loudly declared,

---

* *A-propos des Bottes*. Two persons talking of wine, somewhat pompously, in the presence of another, who for some reason or other, (guess) had not cracked a bottle for a long time before that, he exclaimed, "A-propos of wine! here, waiter, bring me *a pipe*." But he meant *a pipe of tobacco*; for the arch wag intended to *smoke* the two bouncers.

Encore:—A-propos *des bottes*,
Apportez moi une Omelette,
Si non, Monsieur, un Matelot.

"missing" by their rightful owners; but the rogues mustered in such force upon every remonstrance of the sort, that the barest attempt at recovery would put the robbed persons in danger of their lives. It has been suggested, that when such assemblages take place, "if the police-officers would attend at the turnpikes, or avenues leading into town, they might catch the robbers and the plunder together." To this advice we may, not improperly, add, from our own observation, that the booty is generally borne to London in little carts, in which a woman or two has been stationed during the fight, to receive incontinently the ill-gotten deposits.

THE FIGHT.

Tom Hickman sustained the character he has already acquired, by again licking Cooper in *double quick time*. Cooper, it will be recollected, never trains well, requiring rather generous aliment; and, in his journey from Edinburgh to London, is said to have found his legs incommoded with certain tumours, occasioned by the want of vigour in his general habit.

Cooper is a good two-handed hitter, his *one-two* being planted in the very best Belcherian style; but we could not fail to notice, that he is too old by a dozen years for his antagonist, —years that constitute the primest of a man's life, and in passing to or from which, one man may be said to be fighting *downwards*, the other *upwards*: or, in other words, one is daily getting older and better, the other older and *worser*. It is remarkable, that all George Cooper's fights were of short duration; that with Molineux being one of the longest, scarcely exceeding twenty minutes; with Oliver seventeen;* whilst Jay was finished by him in eight minutes. So did Gas, in their

---

* On that occasion, as on the present, victory was said to have been snatched (or 'stolen') from him at the very moment when he might reasonably have reckoned upon coming off conqueror. Of his fight with Robinson in Scotland, or Donelly in Ireland, we purposely say nothing; we now allude to his contest with Oliver, that our readers may form some judgment of the approaching contest between Tom Hickman and Oliver—both conquerors of Cooper. To our recollection, the blow given by Cooper to Oliver, on the 15th May, 1813, resembled, in every particular, the one he now *received* nearly eight years afterwards—except as to the consequences being different, inasmuch as the *receivers* were in totally different *condition*.

first fight, finish George in little more than fourteen minutes; though we are far from wishing to have it inferred, that he is not nearly as good a man, and quite as good a sparrer as any man of the day.*

Gas-Light is worthy of notice as a rising pugilist, and a good natural fighter; he is also the first man we ever met with who *bragged* and performed his promises too. The phrase, "brag's a good-dog, but holdfast is a better," as a word of reproach, is inapplicable to Thomas Hickman. Buonaparte did the same, and so far as the matter goes with either character, it may be allowable enough. Always overmatched, yet always victorious, there is no saying what he may not do; seven pitched battles, about a score of street-fights, in one of which he licked seven iron-founders, who had way-laid him, who were laughed at by the *beak* himself for their incredible evidence at Union Hall—and all before his fight with Crawley, seem to pave the way to still higher honors than he has yet aspired to. As to Cooper, we entertain no doubt as to the event of any future contest between him and Hickman—*barring accidents*; and allowing every thing the backers of a beaten man may urge in excuse for their defeat, he never will come into the ring with Gas at even betting, or any thing like it, nor maintain the contest half-an-hour. "But the *first blow* given by Cooper was tremendous," say many *fanciers*; but, however, we all know what importance is justly attached to its being well served out upon such a customer as Gas is, yet this is the kind of man in all the world upon whom nothing but the primest execution can have the *desired effect* through the remainder of a battle. On the contrary, any thing short of closing an eye, or disordering the vital part of him, so far from being of any *disservice* to such a receiver, only tends, as in the present case,

---

* His chief defect appeared to lie in his want of *training*, and consequent debility in the digestive and blood-making organs. From the sallow colour of his skin, 'tis evident something or other is the matter with the upper part of his liver, not *schirrous*, but at the biliac duct; and the necessary langour follows of his general system, which requires to be raised by a dry generous diet, constant attention to the primary evacuation, and proper, not too much, exercise. This course would cause the absorption and passing off those humours that at their first appearance alarm the patient, and incommode the muscle on which they arise.

to rouse up every one of his latent energies to the uttermost. Such has been the case in all the pugilists of *heavy habits,* as Bittoon, Cribb, and twenty others we could name, who require "pricking up a bit;" whilst such men as Turner, Randall, and those kind of men, are incited to more forceful exertion as they notice the *impressions* they may leave upon their antagonists.

Gas had been trained in the best manner, under the superintendence of the gentlemen of the Herts Hunt, who patronized him; he accordingly appeared in prime condition, full of confidence himself, and inspiring others with the same feeling. Whereas Cooper's *langour,* or call it the "dilatoriness of his animal system," was evident from the first moment. The consequence whereof was, that his legs were both in an ulcerated state, and his whole body partook of the same evil quality; from which no treatment whatever, probably, can set him *completely* free—though much might be done for him. But all this was not previously known to *the other side,* and therefore they were not borne out in the heavy odds all along offered, viz. 6 to 4, and 7 to 4 occasionally; for no two known men ever were backed, upon which the odds could fairly rise so nearly 2 to 1; and in the present case, we are inclined to attribute it as much to the eagerness of Hickman's friends as to the conscious backwardness of those of George Cooper. The bets, though numerous, were not heavy.

All being ready, shortly after one o'clock Hickman was introduced to the assemblage in form, by one of the Hertfordshire *swells.* He seemed much at his ease, lounged in the right style, and having shortly cast his hat into the roped *square,* doff't his white tog; when we, who were in his rear, discovered a blue bird's-eye *wipe* tied round his *squeeze.* Cooper wore the *yellow*; and, as soon as he had thrown down his *castor,* went up to Hickman, shook hands, and spoke with his usual suavity to his rough antagonist. For him appeared Belcher and Harmer to pick him up, whilst Randall and Shelton performed that office for Gas. Mr. Jackson proposed that two gentlemen should be chosen to whom any dispute that may arise was to be *referred*; and these *Referees,* lest they might not agree chose a

third, who was to act as Umpire between them.* The same
"Master of the Ceremonies" directed the Seconds and Bottle-
holders just named, "that upon the men setting-to they were
all to retire to the corners of the *ring*, and, when TIME was
called, they must immediately bring the men to *the scratch*."
A very proper and needful precaution, not only as regarded
the men in the *square*, but the convenience of the spectators—
to say nothing of the stakes and bets depending upon the contest, and we shall be much gratified at seeing the precaution
persevered in for the future. Upon the present occasion it became the more necessary, in consequence of some rumours
which had gone abroad, as to a rough saying of one of the
seconding-men. Formerly, we recollect, the Seconds would
also fight the Seconds of the adverse party; and, within our
remembrance, many disgraceful tricks were played:—Johnson
contributed to prevent Dan Mendoza from planting a blow on
Humphreys's loins that must have decided the battle, for which
he would, old Broughton observed, in his days, "have been
kicked off the stage, and nothing else." Harry Lee and Mendoza abused Gully most opprobriously in the battle with
Gregson, when the first-mentioned Jew spit in John Gully's
face. This was too bad. Most Seconds make grimaces at their
opponents, and Richmond's harlequin tricks were always
past endurance.

First Round.—Hickman came on furiously; but Cooper showed him the
preventers, hit out, and broke away in good style: he retreated, Gas following
him. At length the latter, in the true spirit of a determined miller with small
science, rushed upon his antagonist, and was received at the moment of hitting
short with his left hand, by the left hand of Cooper on the cheek-bone; it was
the *left* also, and from this circumstance it will be concluded he must be partly
round at the moment, and just in the position for *feeling it*. He went down on
the spot, like one shot; a proof how much may be done by coolness and a
Master of Arts—whilst he is fresh.

Betting became even; some taunts were passed: "Now where's your 7 to 4?
Cooper for a hundred—Gas is done for."

---

* Up to this moment a mistake in terms has been *taught* by the news-caterers, as
regards this part of the *business* of the Ring: our legal coadjutor would recommend,
that the services performed by those gentlemen should hereafter be called "Arbitration,"
and they all three "Arbitrators." Of which, however, *non-constat*, as ——— might say.

Second Round.—But the fallen man got upon his pins again, at the word Time, quite game, though looking very serious. Cooper now fought offensively; but was in turn too eager at first; he hit short several times, in consequence of that piece of forgetfulness; and Gas, nowise backward, bored away at him quite up to the ropes. Here Cooper levelled a blow at the head of Hickman, which, had it told, must have sent him down as before; but the latter returned it with such astonishing force and quickness, that few saw the blow take place, and Cooper flew through the ropes like a pellet from a pop-gun. The hit took place on the jaw-bone, upon his left whisker, near the ear; and must have twisted the glands of the neck, and gone near to dislocate the lower part of the head from the *cranium*: by the former, the blood-vessels, particularly the parotid artery, would be pressed upon, and momentarily cease its function of supplying the heart, and thus account for the temporary absence of life; while by the latter was effected that forgetfulness which rendered the beaten man unconscious of what passed. Those functions having ceased, but returning to their proper exercise in two or three minutes, might have enabled Cooper to fight again without this occurrence having any effect on the physical man, whatever it might on his mental; but, as may be surmised, the *half-minute's* time being lost, lost him the battle, and it could not be renewed on any suit. However, although he could not be lifted off Harmer's knee, but dropped on it again, and the Gas-light-man and his seconds stood ready for a minute to receive him, inquiring whether he was licked already? and when they had taken Gas to his chaise, upon the assurance that this was the case—yet an attempt was made on the part of Cooper's friends to renew the combat. A gentleman dispatched a messenger after the chaise in which Hickman went off, with an offer for him to fight Cooper another fresh battle for £50, and Cooper stood ready and eager to fulfil it; but the thing was inadmissible, as it might have been construed, by many *betters*, into a renewed combat for the original stakes, and thus create confusion. Jack Randall declared it "b———— stuff," and drove home with his man to Chancery-lane, where they arrived at five o'clock.

Never was consternation at the event of a prizefight so eminently depicted on an assembly of Britons: *three* short minutes to dispatch the business of a first-rate man of science, seemed like a fable, for it could not be, seeing he was now ready to set-to again. Every sort of conjecture as to *when*, *where*, and *how* the blow was *given*, *received*, and *told*, was put in motion; all endeavoured to account for its effects, according to his means of judging; and the writer in a weekly paper persuades himself, and wishes his readers to believe, that "a *heavy hit* on this *fleshy part* of the neck might not leave a mark," [scrag of mutton *to wit*.] Yes, it would though, or a *slight* one either, although the part is not *fleshy* at all, but replete with *glands*, which always show the effects of contusion. So much for ————'s explanation in an anatomical *point of view*, as he calls it; which puts us in mind of a fellow who reads the word "a-no-tomical."

Under circumstances, perhaps, we may consider it a God's mercy, that, during the time Hickman waited for him, Cooper did not so far recover as to be *just enabled* to face his man: for in that case it is more than probable he might have been in such a state of body as not to have made the requisite efforts— and so affected in mind as to have exposed himself to another such attack, as would probably have sent the life completely out of him.

Men with short necks, and full of blood, are very liable to similar short suspensions of life, and from very trivial, or non-immediate, causes. About three years ago, we recollect, Tom Cribb received such a visitation, after having dined heartily.* He was at the time in the Castle Tavern, and a long while elapsed (near a minute,) before the people present, by giving new impulse to the blood, could recover the Champion from his stupor. After awhile Tom Belcher called out "Time! Time!!" and the pluck of the suffering man enabled him to get up, with "I'm ready;" but *two or three minutes* passed away before every thing within recovered its wonted course, and he was enabled to resume the conversation. If, during those two or three minutes, he had really been brought to face a man, who can doubt the result? So with Cooper during the time of his blood recovering *its* wonted course; for although the *cause* was very different, the effect was brought about by the very same means, *viz.* the sudden cessation of the circulation by the jugular vein into the parotid artery.

Sporting Ardour—The late Duke of Grafton, when hunting, was thrown into a ditch; at the same time a young curate, calling out, "Lie still, my Lord," leaped over him, and pursued his sport. Such an apparent want of feeling, we

---

* Dr. Kitchener considers all such attacks upon our safety, ease, or comforts, as so many rebukes given by nature to our indulgences, our excesses at table, or neglect of nature's calls in another respect: had the good fellow, named in the text, taken one of the doctor's "Peristaltic Persuaders" at dinner-time, 'tis 7 to 1 he would not have thus made blood so fast as to stop up the passage to the heart.—*See "Peptic Precepts."*

may presume was properly resented. No such thing: on being helped out by his attendant, his Grace said, "That man shall have the first good living that falls to my disposal: had he stopped to have taken care of me, I never would have given him any thing:" being delighted with an ardour similar to his own, or with a spirit that would not stoop to flatter.

FEMALE TURN-UP.—JENNINGS *v.* EVANS.—Mrs. Mary Evans was brought before the sitting magistrate, at Bow Street, on Tuesday se'nnight, by Smith of the patrol, on a warrant charging her with an assault on the person of Miss Jemima Jennings.

Mrs. Mary Evans is a tall thin matron, somewhat declining into the vale of years; but her countenance—especially the most prominent part of it, which is very prominent indeed—still blooming with spirituous comforts. Miss Jemima Jennings is a very pretty mild-spoken young woman, with a countenance blooming with youth.

Miss Jemima deposed, that on a certain day named, she *happened* to be going along a certain street, and, as the weather was very hot, she *happened* to go into a certain public-house, to take a glass of Henry Meux and Co's entire. She there *happened* to see a gentleman who very politely asked her to take a glass of something short, telling her it would *squench* her thirst better than porter. She resisted his invitation for some time; but, at length she consented to take a glass of short—a cool *dodger* of *cloves and brandy*; and, having drank it, she thanked the gentleman for his politeness, and went on her way—pretty considerably refreshed. Next day, she *happened* to go into the same public-house again—not with any expectation of meeting the same gentleman again, but with the sole intention of taking a dodger of cloves and brandy on her *own* account—she having derived great comfort from the one she took on the preceding day. It so *happened* that the gentleman was not there; at which she was very much pleased; for she could not 'bear the *highdear* of being *beholding* to a gentleman two days together.' Well, whilst she was taking her cloves and brandy, thinking of nothing at all but how very nice it was, who should come in but the defendant, Mrs. Evans, with an 'I want to speak to *you*, young woman.' Now she, Miss Jemima, thought this very comical, for the lady was a perfect stranger to her. However, she followed her up one street and down another, till, at last, Mrs. Jennings opened the door of a house, and said, 'Pray walk in, *Mem*;' and in she did walk, wondering what all this could mean. Mrs. Evans having closed the door, made her a low courtsey, and said, 'Have the kindness to walk this way, *Mem*;' and Miss Jemima followed her along the passage to an inner apartment, like a lamb to the slaughter-house, as she said; for they had no sooner entered the room than Mrs. Evans seized a *broomstick*, and, without uttering a single word, began to belabour her over the back and shoulders with all her might! Miss Jemima shrieked, or *squeeked*, as she called it, for help; but not a soul came to her assistance; and she was obliged to defend herself as well as she could with her hands alone, till Mrs.

Evans dropped her broomstick for lack of breath; and then she, Miss Jemima, made her way out of the house, covered with bruises and wonder.

This was the unprovoked assault complained of, and for this Miss Jemima Jennings claimed redress at the hands of the law.

Mrs. Evans made a very voluble defence. She was cursed with a husband, she said, who—though she brought him twelve children—was continually hankering after other women. On Monday last he went out, taking with him six *golden* sovereigns, which she had put by to pay her coal-merchant, and he did not come near home for three whole days. Some of her neighbours told her that he had been seen treating the complainant (Miss Jemima) with cloves and brandy; and she was so *hasperated* at hearing this that she did entice Miss Jemima to her house, and *hansell* her with the broomstick as she had described. In conclusion, she admitted that she was wrong in so doing, but her passion got the better of her judgment, and she hoped his worship would consider that as an excuse. It was very hard, she said, for a woman at her time of life to be neglected for such *kreters*.

The magistrate told her he thought she ought not to have proceeded to such a violent outrage upon the complainant without better proof that she was the cause of her husband's faithlessness: but as jealousy was an ungovernable passion, and as she appeared to repent of her violence, he would order the warrant to be suspended for a day or two, in the hope that she would in that time make her peace with the complainant, and save herself further trouble and expense.

————

AMERICAN MODE OF FIGHTING.—Mr. Palmer, in his travels in 1817, through the United States of America and Lower Canada, thus describes the mode of fighting adopted by the inhabitants; which, in comparison with the English practice of boxing, becomes terrific:—"From the rascality and quarrelsome behaviour of a few of the Kentucky men, the whole people have got a very bad character amongst the sister states, especially for blackguardism, and their manner of fighting, when intoxicated; but this is certainly confined to the lowest, and is optional to the fighters. The question is generally asked— '*Will you fight fair, or take it rough and tumble? I can whip you either way, by G—d!* The English reader knows what fair fighting is, but can have little idea of *rough* and *tumble*; in the latter case, the combatants take advantage, *pull, bite,* and *kick*, and with hellish ferocity strive to *gouge*, or turn each other's eyes out of their sockets! I never saw a *gouging* match, and though often of necessity in the lowest company, never had any one offer to do me *that favour*. I believe it is not so common by any means as is represented: I saw but two men who had been injured by this method of fighting—one had almost lost an eye, and the other, a free negro, was nearly or totally sightless. They both lived on the banks of the Ohio, where this dreadful art is most practised; it was introduced from the Southern States. There certainly ought to be a strong law enacted to prevent a resort to so brutal a practice; surely it is a disgrace and stigma to the legislature. *Prize-boxing* is unknown in the United States."

Memoirs

OF

TOM SHELTON,

THE NAVIGATOR.

———

THIS hero is a native of Wrotham, in Kent, and was born on the 1st of May, 1787. SHELTON is in weight about 12 stone 7 lb. and in height 5 feet 10 inches. He is a scientific boxer—a truly brave man in the ring—a good in-fighter, but a left-handed hitter.

SHELTON'S first regular combat, it seems, took place in St. Giles's Fields, when he was only 16 years of age, with *Jem Germain*. The latter *chap* was not only a taller man, but a stone heavier than SHELTON. It was a most desperate battle, although the sum contested for did not exceed *five shillings* a side. SHELTON proved the conqueror in 40 minutes.

Near the sign of the Prince of Wales, in Webb's brick-field, Tottenham Court Road, SHELTON distinguished himself, in *milling Charles Smith*, and *Jack Goddard* in the course of three rounds. The latter was looked upon as an *out-and-outer*, weighing 15 stone, and, upon his witnessing *Smith* being *served* out in style, he observed, "Let me come at him." But SHELTON gave *Goddard* such a *muzzler*, that he went down like a shot, his heels kicking up in the air. He immediately, upon this occurrence, lost all conceit of himself, and said, he would not fight any more.

Jem Carter was defeated in the short space of twenty minutes, in the road, near the sign of Mother Red Cap, Camden Town. It was a row; and SHELTON, although inebriated, backed himself for five shillings and a gallon of beer.

For seven years, SHELTON, it is said, was the *cock of the walk* about Tottenham Court Road Fields, beating all his opponents.

A big navigator of the name of *Brown*, in Camden Town Brick-fields, having refused to pay a gallon of beer to his companions, SHELTON took up the dispute, and beat *Brown* off hand in four rounds.

SHELTON next agreed to fight *Tom Flanagan*, (a swaggering sort of a *chap*, and a big man, who had insulted all his fellow workmen,) for five shillings and a gallon of beer, near the sign of the Adam and Eve, in the Regent's Park. In the course of nineteen minutes SHELTON proved the conqueror; and *Flanagan* was so terribly *punished* as to be carried off the field. A lieutenant of the navy, who witnessed the battle, was so pleased with the conduct of SHELTON, that he emptied his purse, containing nine guineas, and gave them to our hero.

His next battle took place in Tothill-fields, for ten guineas a side, with one *Fitzgerald*, an Irishman. SHELTON fought under the auspices of *Caleb Baldwin*. *Paddy* was a "big one," weighing upwards of 13 stone. This battle was contested on both sides, for the space of 54 minutes, with much manhood and science, when SHELTON was declared the conqueror. The amateurs, who witnessed the efforts of the navigator upon this occasion, were astonished at the boxing requisites he displayed.

He next entered the lists with *Harry Harmer*, and was defeated.

SHELTON was indicted at the Quarter Sessions for the city of London, on the 14th September, 1812, for assaulting *Croker*, one of the police officers, on the Hampstead-road, a short time previous to the above date, when the defendant was prevented FROM HANGING HIMSELF AT A LAMP-POST! through the interference of this officer.

SHELTON, in company with a staunch *pal*, had determined on a day's *spree* in the country, and the place fixed on was at the delightful village of Hampstead. To fill up the time, there was much fun and *larking* during the excursion, with copious libations of *heavy wet* to prevent the arguments from becoming too *dry*, and also numerous invigorating *flashes* of *Blue Ruin* to give point to the *oratory*.

But the *amusements* were not yet considered altogether com-

plete, and therefore, by way of putting a *finish* to the day, the old pot-house recreation of *gaffing* was hit upon. Fortune tantalized SHELTON with alternate successes for some hours, when, at length, his *luck* turned, and he lost every thing that he possessed about his person—the *blunt* having first vanished, SHELTON's *toggery* followed in succession, and the last desperate stake (having nothing else left) was—HIS LIFE.

The destructive effects of gaming were never seen in a more horrid point of view, than in this transaction between SHELTON and his associate. The desperate conduct of these men (though evidently labouring under a state of inebriation,) exceeds every thing upon record. It is scarcely possible to admit of the reality of the circumstance in question—to witness one man "staking his life," with the most perfect indifference as to the event, and viewing the other equally as *callous*, not only in *winning* the life of a fellow creature with as much satisfaction apparently as he would a piece of inanimate metal, but claiming the performance of the contract, with all the barbarous rigidity of a Shylock, *by having the defendant hanged at the first lamp, on their getting to the road across the fields!*

SHELTON, strange to remark, with the utmost alacrity and cheerfulness, anxious, as he thought, *to do the thing that was right*; or, in other words, to fulfil the character of an *honourable* gambler, with a composure and fortitude that would have done honour to a better cause, ascended to the lamp-post, tied a *Belcher* handkerchief round his neck, which he affixed, by the command of the winner (his intimate *friend*,) firmly to the post. The handkerchief, however, gave way by the knots getting loose, not being tied by a more skilful Jack Ketch, *and the intended victim dropped—not into* ETERNITY, *but to the surface of the* EARTH!

"Up again, quickly," cries his *friend*, insisting upon the full performance of the condition of the wager; to this SHELTON *assented without the slightest murmur, and again mounted to fix the knots more securely!*

While in this act, *Croker*, the officer, accidentally passed the spot, and immediately interposed, *sans cérémonie*, with the cudgel he held in his hand, and gave SHELTON several hard blows that brought him to the ground before he could accomplish the SECOND SUSPENSION! For this humane interposition—this stepping-in between a man and ETERNITY, with all his imperfections upon his head, *Croker* was requited with a pair of *black eyes*, and his *nose broken*!

It was for this breach of the peace, that SHELTON was now placed at the bar; and, after the case was fully proved against him, he called witnesses to prove that *Croker* had first struck him three times before he retaliated, adding that the officer had not shewn his staff of authority before he had struck him, and insisting that he had a right to hang himself, *as he lost the wager, and it would have been considered unfair if he had not fully performed the bet! ! !*

After the chairman had observed upon the folly and obstinacy of SHELTON in accusing the officer for preventing the impious act of *intended suicide*, the jury returned a verdict of *guilty*.

Upon the sentence being promulgated, the wife of SHELTON addressed the bench, stating, that from this prosecution she was ruined in her little shop and business, and her four young children were deprived of the means of subsistence, which had cost her no less than 18*l.*, and left her unable to defray farther expenses, in case the sentence should require it: but added, that excepting some such irregular fits and frolics, he was a good husband, and laborious and attentive to his duties.

The bench, in consequence of the good character given of her "lord and master" by the female pleader, were induced to grant SHELTON his immediate liberation.

MISCELLANEOUS.

Westminster Pit.—On Thursday, May 16, Mr. Martin of Galway, presented a petition from the inhabitants of Clerkenwell, to the Honourable Commons in Parliament assembled, praying that the House would adopt some measure for protecting animals from the cruelties to which they were often subjected. The honourable Member said there was a place in this city called the "*Westminster Pit,*" which was appropriated to the exhibition of combats between different animals. Round this pit were congregated a set of the greatest vagrants that ever existed. He had heard it remarked, that Parliament ought not to interfere with the amusements of the lower orders; but he denied that the populace assembled in any considerable numbers round the "Westminster Pit;" it was attended by the very lowest miscreants. Printed bills of the amusements of the "Pit" were distributed, and tickets of admission were sold. One of the printed bills ran as follows:

"*Jacco Maccacco*, the celebrated monkey, will this day fight *Tom Cribb's* white bitch *Puss*. (*A laugh.*) *Jacco* has fought many battles with some of the first dogs of the day, and has beat them all, and he hereby offers to fight any dog in England of double his own weight." (*A laugh.*)

The battle advertised in this bill took place, and after having continued for upwards of half an hour, it terminated by *Puss* tearing away the whole of the under jaw of *Jacco*, who, on his part, lacerated the windpipe and the *arteria cartoidis* of *Puss*. (*A laugh.*) In this state the animals lived for two hours, and then they died. (*A laugh.*) He would be the last man living to interfere with what might properly be called the amusements of the people, but scenes such as he had described could afford pleasure only to the lowest and the vilest of mankind. (*Hear.*) He once went to see the "Pit," and there he saw one of the miscreants, a woman, who belonged to it, who had just returned from the hospital, where she had been confined for six months, on account of a wound which she had received from a bear; for an animal of that kind was kept at the "Pit," besides fifty or sixty badgers. (*A laugh.*)—The way in which the woman received her wound was this: she was passing the bear one day, when the animal gave her a claw and completely scalped her. He hoped that his Hon. Friend, who had introduced a bill for regulating the Police of the Metropolis, would bring the "Pit," within the purview of that measure.

Mr. Lockhart said a few words in support of the prayer of the Petition.

Mr. H. Gurney reprobated the transactions which took place at the "Westminster Pit". He was opposed to interfering with the amusements of the lower orders, but he did not believe that the scenes which took place at the "Pit," were exclusively patronized by the lower orders. The Hon. Member for Galway had said, that he had visited the "Pit," and he might, perhaps, tell the House how many Members of Parliament he saw there. (*Hear.*)

Confab. respecting the Fancy Sports of the Rich and the Poor.

In allusion, we apprehend, to the above parliamentary discussion the following pithy dialogue took place about a fortnight ago, between *Mr. M——n*, of *G——y*, and *Charley Eastup*, the worthy proprietor of the Westminster Pit. It gives very lively but contrasted pictures of the pleasures of the higher and the lower classes.

Mr. M——n. I want to see the animals which you bait at this pit.

Charley. Certainly, Sir (bowing and leading Mr. M. into the pit).

Mr. M. What's your name, pray?

C. Lord, Sir, don't you know *Charley Eastup*.

Mr. M. Why, not exactly. Well, what have you got here?

C. Vy, Sir, there's the bear, and a precious buffer of a good un he is; there's ne'er a dog in Westminster can do him a hinjury. There's three badgers in their boxes; shall I show you vun, Sir?

Mr. M. Yes, do.

C. There, Sir, look at that pretty fellow. He's a precious cutter, I can tell you. He's one of the give and take sort; none o' your turn tails that. Vy, Sir, you'll hardly believe it, but that dog badger was drawed more than two hundred times last Vensday was a week, and now he's as lively as a half skinned eel.

Mr. M. What do you mean by drawed?

C. Lord, Sir, don't you know? Vy, you see, ve puts the badger into this here long box with the door at one end. Then I stands by the box and opens the door, and he that backs the dog drops on one knee, holds him by the skin of the neck with his left hand, and by the tail with the right hand. Then he looses the left hand, and lets the dog in at the badger. Then the dog catches hold, if he's worth the crack of a louse; the man pulls him out by the tail, badger and all; I catches hold of the badger by the tail; the man pops the dogs tail into his mouth and gives it a gripe; the dog lets go; the badger flies up as I pull him, and I give him a neat twist into the box again, and flaps to the door. That's vat ve calls a draw.

Mr. M. Well, it's horribly cruel. I can't think how you can like it.

C. Lord, Sir, it's not cruel; the're used to it. I see you're not one of the fancy, Sir, and so you can't understand these things; but I'll just tell you all about it. You see I keeps this pit, with a bear and two or three badgers, and two or three hack dogs, (a hack dog means one that's kept to shew sport when there's not enough good uns amongst the company). I baits two nights a week, Mondays and Vensdays. I charges six-pence a piece and let 'em bring what dogs they likes; only on match nights, ven there's particular sport going on, I takes a shillin from a poor man, and gentlemen such as you, Sir, gives just what they likes.

Mr. M. God forbid!

C. Vell, Sir, ven the sport begins, the first thing they have is set-to's. Do you know what that is?

Mr. M. God forbid!

C. Vy that means, any two as likes it matches their dogs for a turn up.

Mr. M. A turn up! what's that?

C. Lord, Sir, I see you're quite an infant; vy a fight, Sir, vun vith the other; vat else should it mean? either from the scratch, or as they like it. Vell, ven the're all satisfied with that, I pulls out the bear, and those that likes runs at him.

Mr. M. Runs at him! I should be sorry to run at him. *(Here the bear roared lustily for his dinner. Mr. M. started to the door of the pit, and with some anger, exclaimed)*—Come, Sir, don't impose upon me; I should like to see the man that would run at that bear.

C. Hah! hah! hah! Don't be frightened, Sir, he's as quiet as a cosset lamb. Lord, Sir, how hignorant you must be. It's dogs that runs at him, not the men.

Hah! hah! hah! Oh, Lord, I wish Jack Goodlade and Jos vas here, how they vould laugh. Vell, Sir, I'll tell you all about it. The dogs runs at the bear till they've had enough, and they soon get enough of him, for he's a rum un. Then I shuts him up and brings out the badger-box, and them that likes draws two or three times a piece, (not the men, Sir, you understand, but the dogs or bitches may be, for it's all vun if they're of the right sort.) Ven they've all had a turn, I shuts up the box, blows out the lights, and every body goes away.

Mr. M. But you have not convinced me that this sport is not cruel. Of course the dogs bite the bear and badgers dreadfully, and they bite the dogs.

C. Vy yes, Sir, they all bites as well as they can; but they don't hurt vun another, and ven they do, vy there's no help for it. The monkey (poor fellow! Oh, Sir, I've lost the best hanimal that ever came to this pit—poor Jacko!); he was the chap to bite: but they took all the bite out of him last Vensday— that damned dog pulled off his under jaw, and he was as dead as mutton in half an hour. Howsomever the dog died too, that's one comfort.

Mr. M. Why, was he bit too?

C. Yes, Sir, indeed he was. Poor Jacko cut his vinepipe in two as clean as a vistle, and so he kicked the bucket five minutes after poor Jacko died in my arms.

Mr. M. Monstrous! I'll bring this before Parliament.

C. Oh Lord, Sir! pray don't; you'll ruin me; I've trouble enough with them officers from Queen-square, and they'd soon stop my trade if they didn't like a bit of sport as well as any of the fancy.

Mr. M. I tell you what, Eastup, if you continue this horrible, cruel, abominable, infamous, degrading, monstrous, sanguinary trade, I will bring you before Parliament.

C. Oh Lord, Oh Lord.—Oh, Sir, I'd rather be crammed into the badger box and be baited for a veek. Vy, Sir, you vudent take a poor man's bread from him. Vere's the harm, I shou'd like to know, in a bit of a bait? It keeps many a poor man from vurse. Vy, Sir, it's the poor man's *amusement.* He can't go to your hopperas, and plays, and balls, and all the fine sports that you gentlemen has, and so ven he's done his vork, he just comes here with his bit of a tyke to see vich will get the best of it, his dog or the badger, and if his dog draws vell, Sir, he's as pleased as vun of your great horroters ven the Parl't men cries Hear, hear, hear! to one of his famous speeches about the taxes. Vy, Sir, I dare say you goes to hear the singers at the hoppera, and I'm told that some of *them* loses vurse than an under jaw to make them sing vell. But it's not cruel ven a gentleman's in the case. Vy, Sir, I buys my badgers of a man as brings 'em out of Sussex, and he tells me that you gentlemen breeds all sorts of hanimals on purpose to kill 'em for sport. Vat's a bear and a badger or two, or my poor Jacko, to all the hares, and foxes, and partridges, and pheasants, that you gentlemen hunts, and shoots, and vounds, and vurries, all for your sport?

Mr. M. Let me interrupt you, Mr. Eastup; let me tell you that if there were no sport for the gentlemen on their estates, they would spend all their money in London, and away from home, and the poor would suffer very much.

C. Lord, Sir, not they; vy my friend Vill Hunt tells me as two poor men vas hung at Vinchester, because they happened to kill a gamekeeper belonging to vun of your gentlemen in a row, vich vas caused by their looking after a hare or two, vere there vas so many that the farmers vas eat up vith em. Vy, Sir, its a temptation to poor men ven they see so many things to satify their hunger, runnin about in the voods as thick as peas, and all kept just to give the gentlemen the pleasure of killing 'em. Vy, Sir, your sport brings people to the gallows, it teaches 'em to steal and fight, and commit murder. Vats a bear and badger, or two to that, I should like to know? Its like a milk valk to Rhodes's farm. Then, Sir, you've hopperas, and plays, and balls, and clubs, and horses, and carriages, and boats, and billiards, and books, and larning, and pictures, and a million of amusements, vile the poor man in Lunnun has no sport but a bit of a bait or drinking at the public house; and I should like to know vhich is the best.

Vy, Sir, there's only three or four pits in all Lunnun, and probable they kill a bear or two a year, and a hundred badgers, and twenty or thirty dogs. Vats that to vat vun of you gentlemen does by himself? Vy, Sir, I've been told as vun gentleman kills two hundred things in a day, and vounds a hundred more as dies in the voods of mortification, vith broken legs and vings, and as millions and millions of foxes, hares, pheasants, and partridges are hunted, and shot, and vounded every year by the gentlemen, ven they have plenty of other things to go to, and if its wrong, ought to know it vith all their larning.

Then there's the fish, Sir, vy you gentlemen don't mind hooking a fish, and cutting the hook out of his throat with your pen knives with your own vite hands, and some of the fish escapes vhen the line breaks, and goes away and dies in a hole vith the hook in their guts. Besides, the poor vorms, Sir. Oh, Lord, don't talk to me about poor Jacko and bit of bait; vy its nothing to your sports, Sir, as you all brags and boasts of so much, that he's the best of you as kills and vounds the most things in a day; poor tame things, as you breeds and feeds on purpose to take their lives away only for sport and fun, just to have the pleasure of counting how many you have killed.

Mr. M. Why, *Mr. Eastup*, you are quite eloquent, but you don't understand the thing. If you had an education you would see the difference, between the healthy, exhilarating, honourable sports of the field, and these atrocious, dreadful, heart-rending amusements.

C. Lord, Sir, don't tell me; I can see a pike-staff without a hedication; but I'm a poor man, and mine's a poor man's amusement. So you fine gentlemen don't like it, tho' its not half so cruel as yours. Vy, Sir, I begin to think you must have been joking ven you talked about the Parliament. Vy, Sir, I'm told as all the sporting gentlemen are Parliament men, and makes laws on purpose to keep the game for them to torture to death; not a nasty bear, and a few stinking badgers a-year, but millions and millions of poor, clean, beautiful

hares and rabbits, and fine birds, as they breed in cages on their lawns, and turns out in the voods on purpose to shoot at, just for sport. Oh, Lord, Sir, don't talk to me about cruelty.

Mr. M. (very angrily.)—I'll bring you before Parliament. I'll put a stop to this horrible system. You impertinent puppy, how dare you talk to me this way? You shall hear more of this. *(Exit Mr. M.)*

Charley (alone.)—Vy d—n that feller's eyes. He is a pretty chap indeed. Vel, if he takes me before Parliament, I'll tell 'em a bit of my mind; but I believe I'd better let it alone, for I'm a poor man, and they are gentlemen.

———

'LIFE IN LONDON,' What is it?—We are led to make this inquiry, in consequence of some attempts lately made at depicting 'Life in London,' which do not square with our notions of what the thing ought to be. But, probably, we do mistake those gentlemen egregiously; they do not *mean* to depict (to paint) *actual life,* but merely to set forth a pretty print, 'a study' of the brain, and to give the gaping world a new species of the *beau-ideal,* that exists no where but in their own sconces. We are borne out in this conclusion (somewhat) by the very names they give to their fictitious *heroes,* in which they furnish us with a foretaste of the caricature situations and unheard-of scenes, in which they subsequently throw their said HEROES. 'Heroes?' Yes; for every thing they take in hand becomes heroic, or monstrous fine, tremendously inconceivable,* or excessively superb.

Is it to describe Life in London, *as it actually is,* to write a fiction full of bombastical absurdities? Is it set forth such as it ought to be, when flights of poetry, fifty years old, are dragged in neck-and-heels from the *shelves,* to narrate seeming facts and occurrences! which facts, by the way, *never happened,* but are lies, lies, lies, from beginning to end, or 'False as Hell,' and ugly as Hecate, to boot. Is it not any thing but "Life," that when a bit of truth chanceth to slip in, it is then hung up in the clouds—or compelled to float in the hazy atmosphere of the writer's caprice, or held up by tortuous ponderosity in the sun's eye, evidently for the purpose of scorching the reader with its beams?

As an example of the latter—would any one of common sense, any one of the ten thousand readers of our FANCY, imagine, that such men as we and they are (for example), or any of our acts, would be appropriately introduced to public notice by such blazing lines as these—

> "Oh for a Muse of fire, whose burning pen
> "Records the God-like deeds of valiant men!
> *   *   *   *   matchless hero," &c.

And who, what "matchless hero," does the reader imagine, causes this effulgency? Why, no other than George Hanger! Honest *George,* who desires us to declare the whole passage ——— "all slum, by God! Tell them so, my Chick of *the Fancy,*" enjoined our old acquaintance.

———

* In America such authors receive the name of "Jargonic Writers."

After this exposition of what 'Life in London' is *not,* let us see what it actually is: it is to depicture ACTUAL LIFE IN LONDON, aright, when the reader is led to an intimate acquaintance with the FANCY SPORTS of the Metropolis, their corollaries and minor incidents. It is actual life in London, *as it passes,* that is depicted in the numbers of THE FANCY; which contain the *occurente laborem,* the practical experience of our active lives, devoted to the Task, and revelling in a fearless search after Truth. Aided by a galaxy of talent adapted to every one of its purposes, Life in London is actually seen by us and our very respectable colleagues daily and nightly, hourly and extensively, and it is constantly developed in this our publication. Not recoiling under a cloak of fictitious characters, not conveyed in vague and smoky phraseology, neither doubtful occurrences, or incidents *in nubibus,* disgrace our pages; but straight forward run-and-read lingo, aimed right at the *mark*; real, actual *bona fide* acts, names, transactions; conveying instruction, and imparting precautions and advice, combining information and utility, to every Fancy reader. From this labour, whenever we retire—for *retire* we must and shall, sooner or later—no doubt exists that we shall not only leave *the ring* in a better moral state, and more tolerable, than when we came into it, but that the public and the magistracy, and the governors of the land, will understand better the objects, aims, and acts of the admirers of Fancy Sports, as pursued in this capital of the Empire. N.B. More proofs hereof in the next Number.

———o◯o———

POLL EARLY, an equivoque.—At the late general election, the candidates for London daily appealed, by large posting-bills, for support, to their fellow-citizens. One of these bills, of immense size, contained only "*Poll Early* for Alderman Wood," in very large characters. Now it happened that a fair Cyprian, Miss Hurley, of the Spice Islands, in Grubstreet, who had been christened ('tis supposed,) Mary, but who could not read her book the best in all the world, was induced by some one who knew a *little more,* to take umbrage at this large bill: "Poll Hurley" (early,) said her friend, "damn it, don't you see they've got you up, in *print.*" Poll was terrified at being IN PRINT, as most shallow-headed people are—in fact she would sooner appear in Bridewell, for then, as she observed, "a body knows the worst on't: a month does it; and then the citting Alderman may ——— my rump," she added, vulgarly. But to be stuck up all over town, printed and reprinted, and entered at Stationers' Hall; to be stitched and folded, and beat, and to be boarded, and bound and rebound, and cut-up, and all that, 'tis too bad; many, very many, in higher life than Poll, kick at it, and so did she. But what could *she* do with an Alderman?—a beak? No more, we apprehend, than ——— ——— could do with us, *in any way:* she could *blow up,* however, and that *well*; so down to Cateaton-street went she, accompanied by all the fillies and fancy-coves from that prolific neighbourhood, and also as many Long-alley Lads of the Village and their Molls, as could turn out of their dabs at that early hour (11 a. m.). She protested, with many an oath, that slipped out of her ruby lips in conse-

quence of pressing her ribs on each side, which relieved the workings of her diaphragm, and assisted the action of the metacarpal muscles, whilst at the same time it enabled her to show fight, in arms a-kimbo, to "the committee up stairs," as they say in the House—she protested "she never had any thing to do vith Alderman Vood, whatever, nor he vith me." One of the gentlemen endeavoured to *spell* her into good-humour, but she declared it all gammon, and appealed to her mother and her aunt, and her aunt's sister-in-law, and her cousin Jack (Hurly, being the orthography always used of him by the clerk of arraigns,) and to all who had known her since she was no higher than a quartern of gin, that she never cared about spelling: "Then, vhy should any body as happens to be poor, or in *the vay of life*, be put upon by this Alldeman Vood; so help me Bob!" added she, "I never saw the colour of his money in all my born days, nor the colour of any thing he has *(a laugh)*; nor I don't care for him, nor for any on you—there now!" She concluded by snapping her two bunches of fives together in succession, while all the Spice-Island and Long-alley colonists, there present, gave their hearty assent in *the usual manner*, i. e. between a howl, a hoot, and a huzza, accompanied by the finger-whistle. Then did Mary, sweet Mary, bring her thieving-irons together with such wondrous force, that some one taking the hint she had given, put something into her hands, as much in the shape of half-crowns as possible, and she departed *the place* then, and England soon after, in consequence of somebody's bother about a swell's fawney.

To our *Fancy*, the story of Poll Hurley resembles as much the beginning, carrying on, and termination of an action for libel, as possible; and we would explain how, had we not a very exalted idea of the reader's judgment and discretion in those particulars, which seem to render that labour a work of supererogation.

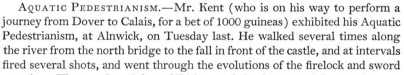

AQUATIC PEDESTRIANISM.—Mr. Kent (who is on his way to perform a journey from Dover to Calais, for a bet of 1000 guineas) exhibited his Aquatic Pedestrianism, at Alnwick, on Tuesday last. He walked several times along the river from the north bridge to the fall in front of the castle, and at intervals fired several shots, and went through the evolutions of the firelock and sword exercises. The novelty of the exhibition, and the fineness of the evening, attracted a very numerous assembly to witness this singular spectacle.—Mr. Kent made a similar exhibition at Berwick on the King's birth-day.

FANCY ARTICLES, in America: *Advertisement.*—Jacob Moss is sorry that his intemperate zeal induced him to interrupt the Rev. Mr. Frey, on Friday, at the Presbyterian church. He hopes the Baltimoreans will accept this apology. J. M. has the honour to inform his friends of Baltimore, that he has arrived from Philadelphia with a large quantity of FANCY ARTICLES, which are to be sold on the most reasonable terms.

On the Advantages

of

TRAINING.

═══

THE art of Training for athletic exercises consists in purifying the body, and strengthening its powers by certain processes, which thus qualify a person for the accomplishment of laborious exertions. It was known to the ancients, who paid much attention to the means of augmenting corporeal vigour and activity; and, accordingly, among the Greeks and Romans, certain rules of regimen and exercise were prescribed to the candidates for gymnastic celebrity.

The manner of Training among the ancients bore some resemblance to that now practised by the moderns. But as their mode of living, and general habits were somewhat different from those of the present age, a difference of treatment is now required to produce the same effect.

The skilful trainer attends to the state of the bowels, the lungs, and the skin; and he uses such means as will reduce the fat, and at the same time invigorate the muscular fibres. The patient is purged by drastic medicines; he is sweated by walking under a load of clothes, and by lying between feather-beds. His limbs are roughly rubbed; his diet is beef or mutton; his drink is strong ale; and he is gradually inured to exercise, by repeated trials in walking and running.

The most effectual process for *training*, is that practised by Captain Barclay; and the particular mode which he has adopted has not only been sanctioned by professional men, but has met with the unqualified approbation of amateurs. The following statement, therefore, contains the most approved rules; and it is presented to the reader, as the result of much experience, founded on the theoretic principles of the art.

The pedestrian who may be supposed in tolerable condition, enters upon his Training with a regular course of physic, which consists of three doses. Glauber's salts are generally preferred; and from one ounce and a half, to two ounces are taken each time, with an interval of four days between each dose. After having gone through the course of physic, he commences regular exercise, which is gradually increased as he proceeds in the training. When the object in view is the accomplishment of a pedestrian match, his regular exercise may be from twenty-four miles a day. He must rise at five in the morning, run half a mile at the top of his speed up hill, and then walk six miles at a moderate pace, coming in about seven to breakfast, which should consist of beef-steaks, or mutton-chops under-done, with stale bread and old beer. After breakfast, he must again walk six miles at a moderate pace; and at twelve lie down in bed without his clothes for half an hour. On getting up, he must walk four miles, and return by four to dinner, which should also be beef-steaks or mutton-chops, with bread and beer as at breakfast. Immediately after dinner, he must resume his exercise by running half a mile at the top of his speed, and walking six miles at a moderate pace. He takes no more exercise for that day, but retires to bed about eight, and the next morning proceeds in the same manner. After having gone on in this regular course for three or four weeks, the pedestrian must take a *four mile sweat*, which is produced by running four miles in flannel, at the top of his speed. Immediately on returning, a hot liquor is prescribed, in order to promote the perspiration, of which he must drink one English pint. It is termed the SWEATING LIQUOR, and it is composed of the following ingredients: viz. one ounce of caraway seed, half an ounce of coriander seed, one ounce of root liquorice, and half an ounce of sugar-candy, mixed with two bottles of cyder, and boiled down to one half. He is then put to bed in his flannels, and being covered with six or eight pair of blankets, and a feather bed, must remain in this state from twenty-five to thirty minutes; when he is to be taken out and rubbed perfectly dry. Being then well wrapped up in a great coat, he walks out gently for two miles to breakfast, which, on such occasions, should consist of a roasted fowl. He afterwards proceeds with his usual exercise. These sweats are continued weekly, till within a few days of the performance of the match, or, in other words, he must undergo three or four of these operations. If the stomach of the pedestrian be foul, an emetic or two must be given, about a week before the conclusion of the *training*, and he is now supposed to be in the *highest condition*. Besides his usual or regular exercise, a person under Training ought to employ himself in the intervals in every kind of exertion which tends to activity, such as cricket, bowls, throwing quoits, &c. that, during the whole day both body and mind may be constantly occupied.

The DIET or REGIMEN is the next point of consideration. Animal diet is alone prescribed, and beef and mutton are preferred. The lean of fat beef, cooked in steaks, with very little salt, is the best, and it should rather be under-done than otherwise. Mutton being reckoned easy of digestion, may be occasionally given, to vary the diet and gratify the taste. The legs of fowls are highly esteemed. It is preferable to have the meat broiled, as much of its nutritive quality is lost by roasting or boiling. Biscuit and stale bread are the only preparations of vegetable matter which are permitted to be given. Veal and lamb are never allowed, nor pork, which operates as a laxative on some people; and all fat or greasy substances are prohibited, as they induce bile, and consequently injure the stomach. But it has been proved by experience, that the lean of meat, contains more nourishment than the fat, and in every case the most substantial food is preferable to any other kind.

Vegetables, such as turnips, carrots, or potatoes, are never given, as they are watery and of difficult digestion. On the same principle fish must be avoided, and, besides, they are not sufficiently nutritious. Neither butter nor cheese is allowed; the one being very indigestible, and the other apt to turn rancid on the stomach. Eggs are also forbidden, except the yolk taken raw in the morning. And it must be remarked, that, salt, spices, and all kind of seasonings, with the exception of vinegar, are prohibited.

With respect to liquors, they must always be taken cold; and home-brewed beer, old, but not bottled, is the best. A little red wine, however, may be given to those who are not

fond of malt liquor, but never more than half a pint after dinner. The quantity of beer, therefore, should not exceed three
pints during the whole day, and it must be taken with breakfast and dinner, no supper being allowed. Water is never given
alone, and ardent spirits are strictly prohibited, however di-
luted. It is an established rule to avoid liquids as much as possible, and no more liquor of any kind is allowed to be taken
than what is merely requisite to quench the thirst. Milk is
never allowed, as it curdles on the stomach. Soups are not
used; nor is any thing liquid taken warm but gruel or broth,
to promote the operation of the physic; and the sweating liq-
quor mentioned above. The broth must be cooled in order to
take off the fat, when it may be again warmed; or beef tea may
be used in the same manner, with little or no salt. In the days between the purges, the pedestrian must be fed as usual, strictly
adhering to the nourishing diet, by which he is invigorated.

Profuse sweating is resorted to as an expedient for remov-
ing the superfluities of flesh and fat. Three or four sweats are
generally requisite, and they may be considered the severest
part of the process.

Training for pugilism is nearly the same as for pedestrianism, the object in both being principally to obtain additional
wind and strength. But it will be best illustrated by a detail of
the process observed by Crib, the Champion of England, pre-
paratory to his grand battle with Molineaux, which took place
on the 29th of September 1811.

"The Champion arrived at Ury, on the 7th of July of that
year. He weighed sixteen stone: and from his mode of living
in London, and the confinement of a crowded city, he had
become corpulent, big-bellied, full of gross humours, and
short-breathed; and it was with difficulty he could walk ten
miles. He first went through a course of physic, which consisted of three doses; but for two weeks he walked about as
he pleased, and generally traversed the woods and plantations
with a fowling piece in his hand. The reports of his musquet
resounded every where through the groves and the hollows
of that delightful place, to the great terror of the magpies and
wood pigeons.

"After amusing himself in this way for about a fortnight,

he then commenced his regular walking exercise, which at first was about ten or twelve miles a day. It was soon after increased to eighteen, or twenty; and he ran regularly, morning and evening, a quarter of a mile at the top of his speed. In consequence of his physic and exercise, his weight was reduced, in the course of five weeks, from sixteen stone, to fourteen and nine pounds. At this period, he commenced his sweats, and took three during the month he remained at Ury afterwards; and his weight was gradually reduced to thirteen stone and five pounds, which was ascertained to be his *pitch* of condition, as he would not reduce farther without weakening.

"During the course of his training, the Champion went twice to the Highlands, and took strong exercise. He walked to Mar Lodge, which is about sixty miles distant from Ury, where he arrived to dinner on the second day, being now able to go thirty miles a day with ease, and probably much more, had it been necessary. He remained in the Highlands about a week each time, and amused himself with shooting. The principal advantage he derived from these expeditions, was the severe exercise he was obliged to undergo in following Capt. Barclay. He improved more in strength and wind by his journeys to the Highlands than by any other part of the training process.

"His diet and drink, were the same as used in the pedestrian regimen, and in other respects, the rules previously laid down were generally applied to him. That he was brought to his ultimate *pitch* of condition, was evident from the high state of health and strength in which he appeared when he mounted the stage to contend with Molineaux, who has since confessed, that, when he saw his fine condition, he totally despaired of gaining the battle.

"Crib was altogether about eleven weeks under training, but he remained only nine weeks at Ury. Besides his regular exercise, he was occasionally employed in sparring. He was not allowed much rest, but was constantly occupied in some active employment. He enjoyed good spirits, being at the time fully convinced that he would beat his antagonist. He was managed, however, with great address, and the result corresponded with the wishes of his friends."

Memoirs

OF

TOM MOLINEUX.

"'Tis not a set of features or complexion,
"The tincture of a skin that I admire;
"Beauty soon grows familiar to the lover,
"Fades in his eye and palls upon the sense."

IN taking a view of heroic deeds and valorous achievements in the Pugilistic Ring, it would be injustice to a brave man, to pass the name of TOM MOLINEUX, the tremendous man of colour, whose contest with *Cribb* for the honor of the Championship, gave him an enviable distinction among the competitors for fistic fame, and who, like many of his contemporaries, relying on a naturally good constitution, fell at last the victim of his own improprieties.

TOM MOLINEUX was a native of America, being born in the state of Maryland, in the year 1784, and died in Dublin at the age of 38 years, and he is said to have been descended from a warlike hero who had been the conquering pugilist of that part of the world. Feeling all the animating spirit of his courageous sire, he quitted his native soil in quest of glory and renown, and directed his course to England, "famed for deeds of arms," where his towering disposition and ambitious spirit prompted him to enter the lists with some of the most distinguished pugilists.

On his arrival in this country, unknown, unnoticed, unprotected and uninformed, a perfect stranger, rude and unsophisticated, he offered himself to public notice as a bold and open competitor for boxing fame, resting entirely upon his pugilistic pretensions. In the metropolis he soon attracted the attention of the patrons of those gymnastic sports, and challenged the proudest heroes to the hostile combat. This manly conduct was deserving of respect and attention at least, though it was by many condemned as daring and ambitious in a foreigner, to attempt to wrest the laurels from the English brow; it must, however, be acknowledged his qualifications were of a superior order, and the greatest honor is attached to the conquest of so formidable an hero.

On the first appearance of MOLINEUX in the London ring he was viewed by the English boxers with jealousy, concern and terror; he possessed all the requisites of a modern gladiator, unbounded strength, wind, undebauched, and great agility, with a frame of Herculean mould, his bust was by the best judges of anatomical beauty, pronounced a perfect picture. It was a model for a statuary. He had no high sounding name as a patron to *eclat* his *entrée*, and he *peeled* for the first time on British ground on July 24th, 1810, against a Bristol man of robust make, and about six feet in height, in Tothill-fields.— *Cribb* seconded his countryman, and *Richmond* performed the same office for his coloured friend. The battle lasted for an hour, and was of the gamest description. The *sable hero* punished his opponent so severely that it was impossible to distinguish a single feature of his face, and in the course of the fight he displayed such specimens of dexterity and science, as claimed considerable attention from the *amateurs*, who could not help viewing him as a pugilist of great promise. MOLINEUX was declared the conqueror, and immediately matched to fight *Tom Blake*, a boxer of great repute and practice, who from his fine *bottom* and resolution, was denominated *Tom Tough*.

Within a month after the above encounter the combatants met a few miles from Margate, where this contest was decided on August the 21st, 1810, on the same spot of ground on which *Richmond* and *Maddox* had so bravely contended. MOLINEUX was again seconded by his friend *Richmond*, and *Tom Cribb* did the needful for *Blake*, with *Bill Gibbons* as bottle holder. Eight determined rounds were fought, but evidently in favor of MOLINEUX, so that the brave, the fearless *Tom Tough* became an easy conquest in the hands of his opponent.

The improvement of MOLINEUX in this battle completely

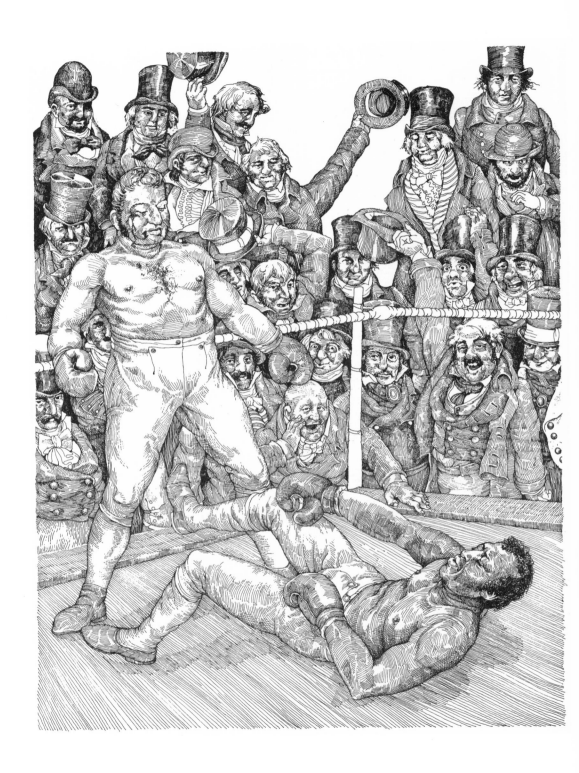

astonished the amateurs, and the *punishment* he dealt out was so truly tremendous, and the strength and bottom he displayed were so superior, that he was considered to be a proper match for the Champion, *Tom Cribb*; a match was accordingly made for 200 guineas, and a subscription purse of 100 guineas for the winner. This match excited considerable interest among the sporting circles. The aspiring ambition of MOLINEUX to become the Champion of England seemed almost to place the honor of the country at stake; and no boxer ever entered the ring with more wishes for his success than *Tom Cribb* had upon this occasion.

The fight took place at *Copthorn*, Sussex, on December 18th, 1810, where *Tom Cribb*, in vanquishing his *brave opponent*, added new laurels to the *Championship*, and honor to his country.

The defeat of MOLINEUX in this contest, however, had not subsided the ardour of his spirits, for in three days after the battle, feeling he was entitled to another chance, he again challenged *Cribb*.

After the defeat of MOLINEUX, a young man of the name of *Rimmer*, a native of Lancashire, about 22 years of age, with stamina and strength of the first quality, and who had distinguished himself in some battles in his own country, was matched against the competitor of the Champion for 100 guineas, under the auspices of *Gregson*, and was contested at Moulsey Hurst in a 25 feet ring, on May 21st, 1811. MOLINEUX, as before, was seconded by his friend *Richmond*, with *Bill Gibbons* for his bottle holder; *Rimmer* was attended by *Powers* and *Jones*.—3 to 1 in favor of MOLINEUX.

In this battle, which occupied 21 rounds evidently in favor of MOLINEUX, a scene took place which beggars all description: during the time *Rimmer* lay prostrate on the ground the ring was broken, owing, it was supposed, to antipathy felt against a man of colour proving the conqueror, if so, the illiberal were completely disappointed by the manœuvre, as those who had taken the odds gained nothing by it, *Rimmer* was exhausted, and almost in a state of insensibility. Confusion was the order of the day, and it would have been a fine subject for the pencil of Hogarth to have delineated. *Corinthi-*

ans and *Costermongers* in rude contact. *Johnny Raws* and *swells* jostling each other, *pugilists* and *novices* all jawing, threatening, swearing and blustering, but no hearing, sticks, whips and fists at work in all directions; ten thousand people in one rude commotion, and those persons in the interior of this vast assemblage suffering all the fatigues of their unsuccessful attempts to extricate themselves from so perilous and unpleasant a situation. This tumultuous scene occupied 20 minutes, till the Champion of England, assisted by some other brave fellows, succeeded in re-forming something like a ring. According to the rules of fighting, if either of the combatants leave the ring he is considered to have lost the battle. MOLI-NEUX and *Rimmer* again *set-to*, and six more rounds were fought, when *Rimmer* was so severely punished as to be unable to stand upon his legs, and consequently acknowledged he had had *enough*.

This and the former battles of MOLINEUX placed him so high on the *milling* list that no pugilist appeared willing to try his powers with this tremendous *man of colour*, till he again entered the list with the *Champion* of England, at Thistleton Gap, in the county of Leicester, on the 28th of September, 1811, in that contest he was again defeated in a much shorter space of time than the former, the battle continuing only *nineteen minutes* and a few seconds. The termination of this fight in favor of *Cribb* was a cause of great exultation to those, who, feeling for the honor of old England, viewed the attempts of MOLINEUX to wrest the laurels of the Champion from his brows with jealousy, envy, and disgust. The mere idea of the national laurels being worn by a foreigner was afflicting, and the reality could not be endured.

This sort of impression, which operated strongly on the feelings of the *Fancy*, rendered MOLINEUX's task more difficult than all the fears he might reasonably entertain, for the well known mighty prowess of his brave opponent, yet it must be acknowledged, that under the disadvantages he had to contend with, he performed wonders, and altho' the prejudice was strongly against him, he had fair play *in the ring* throughout the fight.

It is but justice to remark that great difference existed between the two men, *Cribb* had undergone a most excellent training under the immediate direction of Captain *Barclay*, secluded from the world at the estate of that gentleman, his stamina became invigorated to the finest tone possible, his mind cheerful and independent he entered the ring with a confidence that every chance of success was in his favor; on the other hand MOLINEUX had nothing like a regular training, but indulged himself in excesses far from beneficial to him. His time was exhausted in travelling from town to town to support himself by sparring exhibitions, giving lessons, &c., entering without restraint into all the glorious confusion of *larks* and *sprees* as they presented themselves, and notwithstanding his alleged ferocity he laboured under considerable depression. He was unpopular wherever he went, a circumstance which was considerably heightened on his appearance in the *ring*. His constitution was considerably impaired since the former contest, yet such was the effect of his tremendous efforts, that during the first few rounds of the battle the *flash* side experienced great palpitation.

From the period of this battle, notwithstanding MOLINEUX had publicly challenged all England, he met with no competitor till March 31st, 1813, when a match was made between him and *Carter*, but, as it is reported, *John Doe* and *Richard Roe*, at the suit of *Richmond*, arrested MOLINEUX, in consequence of which the contest did not take place.

MOLINEUX now became an object of attack by boxers of minor pretensions, and Scotland the principal scene of his exploits. Continuing his irregular career of life, it seems he had *gone off* altogether, and at the period of his entering *the ring* with *Fuller*, May 1814, the alteration from what he was at the time of his first appearance against *Cribb* was manifest; when he stript upon that occasion his muscular powers were fine in the extreme. His frame was manliness itself, and his whole appearance terrifically imposing. The anatomist and the artist in contemplating its various beauties, derived an uncommon subject and fine study.

The milling pretensions of MOLINEUX had made a strong

impression on the FANCY in general, and the *nobs* of the boxing circles had endeavoured to console his defeats by liberal
presents, so that although he could not be allowed to wear the
proud title of conqueror to which he aspired, he had little to
complain of on the score of supplies, which the generosity of
the *swells* poured fast in upon him. Thus situated, with a natural taste for gaiety, a strong passion for dress, amorously inclined, and full of gallantry, that the charms of the softer sex
should warmly interest the attentions of the lusty Moor, is
not to be wondered at.

Well *rigg'd* with *togs* of the best quality and *cut*, MOLINEUX
shewed himself as a blade of the first magnitude, and standing
next to the *Champion* of England, which no one could prevent,
he was recognized by many a proud *Corinthian*, conceiving it
no degradation, to know and be known by this renowned *Milling cove*, feeling the power of indulging himself in his pocket
he exercised it with liberality devoid of discretion, and *stews*
of the metropolis not only expeditiously eased him of his *blunt*,
but contributed to undermine a constitution naturally good,
and to impair that overwhelming and terrific impetuosity he
had formerly possessed and conspicuously displayed, and the
consequences of such conduct even the *iron-like* frame of the
Black seriously felt, and evidently shewed. Yet though there
was a visible *falling off* in his appearance, with all his defects he
was not to be *beat off hand*, he was still a formidable opponent.

Fuller, who had been a pupil of *Richmond's*, and whose character for science and game entitled him to every consideration,
fancied himself in every respect able to contend with MOLI-
NEUX, and the amateurs of Scotland, anxious to facilitate a
match between them, subscribed a purse of 100 guineas to be
fought for in a forty feet ring. The combatants met to decide
this contest on Friday 27th May, 1814, at Bishopstorff Peesley,
Ayrshire, about 12 miles from Glasgow. MOLINEUX was seconded by *Carter*, and *Fuller* had the veteran *Joe Ward* and
George Cooper as his attendants.—5 to 4 on the *Black*. At one
o'clock the combatants shook hands, and immediately *set to*.
Good science was displayed on both sides, but when the battle
had continued only eight minutes, the Sheriff of Renfrewshire

entered the ring attended by a *posse* of constables and put an end to it, to the great regret of the combatants, and the disappointment of the spectators. The man of colour was so confident of success that he had betted before the fight five to two he drew the first blood; this bet he won, and also two to one he *floored Fuller* first, the latter was not decided. *Fuller* declared himself in readiness to meet again the next day; MOLINEUX, however, insisted the fight should not take place till the following Tuesday, which arrangement was at length agreed to.

Consequently MOLINEUX and *Fuller* met again on Tuesday the 31st May, at Auchineaux, about 12 miles from Glasgow, on the Drymen road, MOLINEUX attended by an Irish Serjeant of the name of *Haliward* and a Private, and *Fuller* by *Ward* and *Cooper*. The umpires were Captain Cadogan and Mr. George Sterling, with an agreement that in case of any dispute Mr. Guntneaux should act as referee. The battle which took place on this occasion is without parallel. The annals of pugilism can furnish nothing like it. They fought but two rounds in sixty eight minutes. *Fuller* displayed some very good positions, and convinced the spectators that he was a Scientific Boxer. MOLINEUX did not view his opponent with indifference though he flattered himself that *Fuller* must ultimately be defeated. Sparring occupied a considerable time, and much skill was exhibited on both sides, when *Fuller* by a tremendous hit drew the cork of his antagonist, a circumstance which roused the impetuosity of the Black, and he attacked *Fuller* with great ferocity, his endeavours, however, were met by the latter with much adroitness, and *give* and *take* were the orders of the day, a desperate rally succeeded, in which severe milling was dealt out by both parties, when they broke away and again resorted to *sparring* to obtain superiority. *Fuller's sneezer* was strongly *peppered*, and the crimson flowed in abundance. In short, this unprecedented round was filled with rallies, recoverings, retreating, following each other alternately round the ring, stopping, and with various success, and each exhausted by turns, till at length MOLINEUX was *floored* by a tremendous blow, and the round concluded after a lapse of twenty eight minutes.

The second round partook greatly of the nature of the first, but to describe any thing like the various changes which occurred during its continuance, as the veteran *Joe Ward* says, would seem more like the length of Paterson's Road Book than the ordinary round of a fight. It will be sufficient to observe that the whole *minutiæ* of the *milling art* was resorted to from the beginning to the end. The skill, practice, and experience of both the combatants were made use of to the best advantage. *Fuller* proved himself a Boxer of more than ordinary Science and game throughout the fight, and the *Black* was convinced he had a *troublesome* customer to deal with, who required serving out in a masterly style before he could be satisfied. In fact the strength of the *Man of colour* appeared materially deficient of what he had discovered in his former exhibitions when he used to *hit* his man away from him, and levelled his opponent with the most perfect *sang froid*. *Fuller* stuck close to him, and his severe blows made MOLINEUX *wince* again. The *Black* seemed much exhausted by the great portion required for him to *give*, and heartily *tired* of what he was compelled to *take*. Blood flowed in an unusual quantity, and it was supposed *Fuller* lost two quarts in the ring, and his *pimple* was terrific in the extreme, from the dreadful punishment he had undergone, even his seconds lost all traces of his original character. Stauncher *game* was never displayed by any pugilist whatever. Upon the whole it was a truly singular fight, and the people of Scotland witnessed one of the most *nouvelle* specimens of English prize fighting that ever occurred.

The contest, it appears, terminated in rather a singular way. It was asserted by MOLINEUX that *Joe Ward* had acted unfairly, by pulling *Fuller* down at a moment when he was much distressed from having been beaten all over the ring, and by which the *man of colour* was prevented from putting in a decisive blow; upon reference to the umpires it was so decided, and the purse was accordingly awarded to MOLINEUX at the end of the second round, which lasted *forty* minutes.

Notwithstanding the defeat of *Fuller*, his conduct during the battle appears to have given such general satisfaction to the *Fancy*, that a purse of 50 guineas, which had been subscribed for a match between *Cooper* and *Carter*, in consequence of its not taking place, is said to have been presented to him.

MOLINEUX's character still stood high in the consideration of the amateurs of *milling* in Scotland, and he was matched with *George Cooper*, a boxer of acknowledged talent, and on the 11th of March, 1815, a meeting took place between these heroes at Corset Hill, in Lanarkshire, upon which occasion the once tremendous MOLINEUX was defeated in twenty minutes.

A long continued career of *intemperance* had ruined MOLINEUX as a pugilist, and his *punishing powers* were fled, though many a strong commoner who had some ideas of his own talent were made to acknowledge that the *man of colour* was not easily to be *served out*, one of the most remarkable instances of which is related as follows:

While the *sable hero* was on a provincial tour in the year 1813, alighting at the town of Derby for the purpose of exhibiting his *milling* accomplishments to the amateurs and other inhabitants of that place, several *Johnny Raws* had the temerity to try what they could do with the *Black* in a muffled turn up, though they soon discovered they were wrong in reliance on their strength and courage against the skill and science of MOLINEUX. However, a man of the name of *Abraham Denston*, with more of hardihood than his countrymen, possessing the strength of an Hercules, and the size of a Colossus; added to which powerful requisites for boxing, his fame for *milling* was pretty generally known in these parts, as he had successfully encountered some persons who had dared to oppose him. This formidable *miller* entertained an idea, that with the gloves he should be able to *serve out* the Moor in good style, and increase his own fame by the event. Under these circumstances the lads of Derby expected great things from the *countryman*; and considerable interest was excited among the spectators upon their *setting to*. It was, however, quickly allayed, for *Abraham* had evidently over estimated his own abilities, his size and strength were of little avail against MOLINEUX, and two rallies with the *Black* were sufficient to convince him of his error. MOLINEUX *peppered his knowledge box* with great severity, and punished the presuming countryman for his temerity. One of his favorite left-handed lunges gave him such a *remembrancer* under the left *ogle* that the *claret* flew in all directions. This completely spoiled *Abraham's* relish—banished all the *conceit* he previously had of himself, and he made a hasty retreat from the scene of action, amidst the laughter and confusion he had created among the spectators. MOLINEUX and his friend now exhibited some very fine specimens of the art illustrative of the superiority of *Science* when opposed to *mere strength*.

After remaining in Scotland some time our hero went to Ireland on a sparring tour, teaching the warm hearted natives of the *Emerald Isle*, the use of their *mawleys* in preference to their indiscriminate attack with the *Sprig of Shellalah*. Strongly attached to certain old propensities already mentioned and unchecked by reason or reflection upon the consequences of his continual pursuit of intemperate pleasures, he exhausted his muscular powers, and in comparison with his former personal appearance, became little more than a walking skeleton to his once athletic form.

MOLINEUX was so great an object of attraction after his first battle with *Cribb*, that during his sparring tours through various parts of England he was rewarded with hats full of money. His pride was great, and he was remarkably fond of making *a dash*, by entering a country town in a post-chaise and four, ordering the drivers to gallop as fast as possible to the best inn in the place, in order to cut *a swell*, being quite certain that by such proceeding he excited interest and curiosity, enquiry was immediately afloat—"Who is it?" "Where does he come from?" were questions instantly put by the natives, and though some persons might be disposed to laugh at the *trick*, and also to ridicule his presumption, it had the desired effect of bringing numbers to witness his sparring exhibitions. MOLINEUX, notwithstanding his defeats by the *Champion*, entertained a high respect for *Tom Cribb*, which was particularly manifested on one occasion. Such was his desire to serve *Cribb* that he actually came post haste from the potteries in Staffordshire at his own expence, to exhibit at the *Champion's* Benefit at the Fives-court, unknown and unex-

pected by every person, till he absolutely made his appearance on the stage, almost out of breath, and just in time before the conclusion of the sports of the day to have a *set-to* with his old opponent. At another time, in the saloon of the Theatre Royal Covent Garden, accidentally coming in contact with a few *swell covies*, MOLINEUX immediately pulled some of *Cribb's* Benefit Tickets from his pocket, urging that the *Champion* was a good fellow, a brave man, and although he had taken the fight out of him, he was worthy of their support, and that it would also be obliging him (Molineux) if they would become purchasers of *Cribb's* tickets.

A life of dissipation can never be a long one, and we consequently find that the once formidable *man of colour*, who had dared to enter the lists with the *Champion of England*, was *floored* by that universal *leveller*—Death, at Dublin, on the 4th of August, 1821, as before related. The beams of prosperity had long been withheld from him, and for the last four years of his life he was a stroller about the country, existing on the produce of his tuition in the art of self-defence. He died in a room occupied by the band of the 77th regiment, and it was owing to the humanity and attention of three people of *colour* that he was indebted for his existence during the last two months of his life.

BEEF-HEADED BRITONS. *Sparring Extraordinary.*—We did not refuse to take a knife and fork with this amiable Society, on Monday, the 13th of May; and it was a novelty even to us, although, as we were informed *under the tent*, this was "their 20th annual anniversary;" a pleonasm in language we were prepared to *traduct* aright, by reason of our Invitor having previously promised, that "it would be only a three-shilling or'nary upon that Hanni-Wersary of the ———— Britons." But, mark, reader, the uncertainty of our jumble lingo! The *gentleman* meant *beef-eating* Britons; but we were too much elated to think about *spelling* his words, and having so memorandummed the matter, feel too stiffly the verification to alter one *mot*, jot, or iota at the head.

Company—Jolly, blithe, staunch, hearty, cricketty, thirsty: in number 400; handled arms well.

The Day—Inviting, healthy, hilarious.

Place—Highbury-Barn—opened *encore*.

Bill of Fare—Short, but heavy—*videlicet*: Twenty-seven rumps, *boiled*; one hundred and forty ribs, roasted.

Cæteris paribus; cum multiis Aliis,

> "———— shall dissolve,
> And, like the baseless fabric of a vision,
> Leave not a wreck behind."   BILLY.

Notwithstanding Mr. Boniface served up Ox-beef mostly, and the rumps that were not so, came off spayed Heifers; yet there must have been one or two which escaped our notice, derived from more perfect animals. For the company, soon after dinner, became *riggish*, and leap-frog was the order of the day. *Sparring* followed, in the long-room; but *the gloves* having been left at home (and indeed where could be found enough for a hundred men at once), the sets-to were managed without. Such a sight perhaps never was seen before; Waterloo must have been a fool to it—and we wished John Shaw had been here to tell us in what degree. Many good hits aimed, and a few good stops interposed between the greasy-chins and the *punishers*, showed good judgment in both givers and takers. Some few blows *took place*; those upon the bread-basket proving most inconvenient; for "there, in layers, lay the beef and cabbage piled five fingers deep." A wry mouth or two, and a drop of best *max* "to keep it down," closed this part of the amusements, as it does of our report.

————o◯o————

The Position of the Body is of the greatest Consequence in Fighting.

The centre of gravity ought to be well considered, for by that the weight of the body being justly suspended, and the true equilibrium preserved, the body stands much the firmer against opposing force. This depends upon the proper distance between the legs, which is *the first regard a Boxer ought to have*, or all his manly attempts will prove abortive. In order to form the true position, the left leg, must be presented some reasonable distance before the right, which brings the left side towards the adversary; this the right handed man ought to do, that, after having stopped the blow with his left arm, which is a kind of buckler to him, he may have the same readiness and greater power of stepping in with his right hand's returning blow. In this posture he ought to reserve an easy flexion in the left knee, that his advances and retreats may be the quicker. By this proper flexion, his body is brought so far forward as to have a just inclination over the left thigh, insomuch that his face makes a perpendicular or straight line with the left knee; whilst the right leg and thigh in a slanting line, strongly prop up the whole body, as does a large beam an old wall. The body by this means is supported against all violent efforts, and the additional strength acquired by this equilibrium is greatly to the purpose. How much greater weight must not your adversary stand in need of, to beat you back, from this forward inclining of the body, than the so much less resisting reclination of it. By this disposed attitude, you find the whole body gently inclining forward with a slanting direction, so that you shall find from the *outside* of the right ancle all the way to the shoulder, a straight line of direction, somewhat inclining, or slanting upward, which inclination is the strongest position a man can contrive; and it is such as we generally use in forcing doors, resisting strength, or pushing forward any weight with violence, for the muscles of the left side, which bend the body gently forward, bring over the left thigh the gravitating part, which, by this contrivance, augments the force; whereas, if it were held erect or upright, an indifferent blow on the head, or breast, would overset it. The body, by this position, has the muscles of the right side partly relaxed and partly contracted, whilst those of the left are altogether in a state of contraction; but the reserve made in the muscles of the right side is as springs and levers to let fall the body at discretion.

By delivering up the power to the muscles of the left side, which, in a very strong contraction, brings the body forward, the motion which is communicated is then so strong, that, if the hand at that time be firmly shut, and the blow at that instant pushed forward, with the contracting muscles, in a straight line with the moving body, the shock given from the stroke will be able to overcome a force, not thus artfully contrived, twenty times as great.

From this it is evident, how it is in our power to give additional force and strength to our bodies, whereby we may make ourselves far superior to men of more strength, not seconded by art.

Let us now examine the most hurtful blows, and such as contribute most to the battle. *This is a most important consider-*

ation to pugilists and others, and claims their particular attention.
It is well known, that very few of those who fight, know *why*
a blow on such a part has such effects, yet by *experience* they
know it *has*; and by these evident effects they are directed to
the proper parts; as for instance, hitting under the ear, between the eye-brows, and about the stomach. The blow under
the ear is considered to be as dangerous as any that is given,
if it light between the angle of the lower jaw, and the neck,
because in this part there are two kinds of blood-vessels, considerably large: the one brings the blood immediately from
the heart to the head, whilst the other carries it immediately
back. If a man receive a blow on these vessels, the blood proceeding from the heart to the head is partly forced back, whilst
the other part is pushed forwards vehemently to the head; the
same happens in the blood returning from the head to the
heart, for part of it is precipitately forced into the latter, whilst
the other tumultuously rushes to the head, whereby the blood
vessels are immediately overcharged, and the sinuses of the
brain so overloaded and compressed, that the man at once
loses all sensation, and the blood often runs from his ears,
mouth, and nose, altogether owing to the quantity forced with
such impetuosity into the smaller vessels, the coats whereof
being too tender to resist so great a charge, instantly break,
and cause the effusion of blood through these different parts.

This is not the only consequence, but the heart being overcharged with a regurgitation of blood, (as may be said with
respect to that forced back on the succeeding blood coming
from its left ventricle) stops its progress, whilst that part of
the blood coming from the head is violently pushed into its
right auricle; so that as the heart labours under a violent sur-
charge of blood, there soon follows a cardiaca or suffocation,
but which goes off as the parts recover themselves, and push
the blood forward. The blows given *between the eyebrows* contribute greatly *to the victory*; for this part being contused between two hard bodies, viz. the *fist* and *os frontale*, there en-
sues a violent echymosis, or extravasation of blood, which
falls immediately into the eye-lids; and they being of a lax
texture, incapable of resisting this influx of blood, swell al-

most instantaneously; which violent intrimiscence soon obstructs the sight. The man thus indecently treated, and artfully hoodwinked, is beat about at his adversary's discretion.

The blows on the stomach are very hurtful, as the diaphragm and lungs share in the injury.

It is particularly recommended to those who box, *never to charge their stomachs with too much food on the day of combat;* for, by observing this precaution, they will find great service. It will help them to avoid that extraordinary compression on the *etorta descendens*, and, in a great measure, preserve their stomachs from the blows, which they must be the more exposed to, when distended with victuals. The consequence of which may be attended with a vomiting of blood, caused by the eruption of some blood vessels, from the overcharging of the stomach: whereas the *empty stomach, yielding to the blow*, is as much less affected by it, as it is more by its resistance, when expanded with food.

Therefore it is advisable for a man to take a little cordial water upon an empty stomach, which, it is thought, cannot fail in proving of great service, by its astringing the fibres, and contracting it into a smaller compass.

The injury which the diaphragm is subject to from blows which light just under the breast-bone, is very considerable, because the diaphragm is brought into a strong convulsive state, which produces great pain, and lessens the cavity of the thorax, whereby the lungs are, in a great measure, deprived of their liberty, and the quantity of air retained in them from the contraction of the thorax, through the convulsive state of the diaphragm, is so forcibly pushed from them, that it causes great difficulty of respiration, which cannot be overcome till the convulsive motion of the diaphragm ceases.

The scientific boxer may, in some degree, render the blows less hurtful on this part, by drawing the belly, holding his breath, and bending his thorax over his navel, when the stroke is coming.

Strength and art have both been mentioned as the two principal requisites for a Boxer to possess; but there is another equally as necessary, and without which no Pugilist can be termed complete—denominated *bottom*. In establishing *bottom*, there are two things required—*wind* and *spirit*, or *heart*, or wherever you can fix the residence of courage. *Wind* may be obtained by a proper attention to diet and exercise, but it is *spirit* that keeps the boxer upon his legs. Without this substantial requisite both art and strength will avail a man but little.

In tracing thus far anatomically the severe *effects* that blows have upon the human frame, and their ultimate consequences in quickly deciding a contest, or of proving seriously dangerous; little doubt can be entertained, but that, by an attentive perusal of the foregoing remarks, persons, in becoming acquainted with those peculiarly *sensitive parts*, may be enabled, whenever occasion requires, to protect themselves from any threatened danger. This is the ground work of *Science*, and which, in the preceding parts of this work, the reader will perceive practically illustrated, by viewing the Heroes of the Gymnastic Art, and their valorous exploits.

———————o◯o———————

Bull Baiting at Durdham Downs, Bristol.—The bull was led into the ring and tied to the plug a few minutes after our arrival, at this choice and delicious little vale; he walked cooly round the circle, at the full length of his rope, for some time, and then contracting his revolutions by degrees, at length took up his station in the centre of the ring, ever and anon lashing his finely rounded sides with his tail and testily stamping with his fore-foot, as if impatient for the commencement of the fray. A fine two year old dog was the first that was turned in upon him. He rushed up to the bull's head like lightning, and made a desperate snatch at his leather; but the bull, who had placed his curled head close to the turf, and almost between his fore-legs, by a slight, but most effectual jerk, loosened the hold the moment it was effected, and whirled the dog to a very considerable height. He fell, however, within a yard of the bull's heels, and immediately crept, unperceived, beneath his belly, through his fore-legs, and nabbed him by the nether lip. The bull had been looking about to see where his assailant fell, and was somewhat startled at feeling the dog's teeth rioting in his beef so soon again, in a quarter too from whence he least expected him. But in the twinkling of an eye the dog was hurled out of the circle by a desperate uptossing of the bull's head. The noble fellow, however, contrived to elude the many snatches made at him by the spectators, and crawled up towards the death-striking horns again. The bull met him half way, and placing his head askance gored him very severely in the shoulder, and would certainly have sacrificed this fine fellow to his rage, had he not been instantly relieved, and the bull's attention forcibly diverted to another quarter. The play now went on in gallant style; the old bull's head appeared scarcely to move while he sent between two and three dozen dogs successively in the air, to the infinite alarm of their owners, who often essayed to catch them in their arms as they "toppled down headlong" to the earth. Some of the noble-hearted animals, after receiving repeated gores and infuriate tosses, still tottered up to their punisher, and fell under his feet, where they were almost trampled to death, still, however, endeavouring to clutch their terrible opponent by the jowl.

There were as usual a few of the "Jack Rugby," or "follow-my-heel" breed, whose currish propensities were punished with such tremendous and crushing doublers-up, as invariably sent them away hopping on one, two, or three legs (as the case happened), yelping most prodigiously, and turning deaf ears to all the fierce interrogatories and terrific vituperation of their disconsolate and enraged proprietors. The uproar was immense—the gossip of the dogs; the low tones of the bull, growling "curses not loud but deep;" the continual and many-voiced chatter of the ring-clearers as they took away the punished dogs, kept back the heavy-pressing crowd from the reach of the bull's rope; and persuading the many intruding tykes to retire from the circle by dint of most vigorous application to their gridiron ribs, with huge, long, never-to-be-forgotten ashplants, produced such a "concatenation" of noises, as can only be conceived by those who have witnessed some such sport as a prime first-rate bull-bait. "In gude sooth it was a ryghte merrie pastyme."

In the course of the play we observed preparations making at our dexter side, for turning in a fine brindled bitch, with teeth like a wolf's, and an under-jaw projecting far beyond her jet-black quivering nostrils. We think she was just about the prettiest thing in the bull way we had hitherto seen. Indeed we have never since met with above a couple who could match with her in externals. She had been most outrageous since the first dog was uncollared, and there seemed such manifest probability of pinning about her, that we unconsciously said, "that we would individually bet five to seven, that she fixed the roarer."—No sooner had the words slipped over our lips, than a droll-looking old fellow, who was sitting on the ground in our front, cocked up his puckered untonsored iron-grey visage, and stretching out a bony, withered paw, clutched the tip of one of our doe-skin muffles, and, with a satisfied smile, indicative of his self-sufficiency and consciousness of winning, hastily ejaculated "done." This was a closer. We could not retreat if we would. But the chance seemed all in our favour. The bitch was a beauty. There was such palpable breed about her head, and capability of clutching in her under jaw, that the least hint would have induced us to double the bet. Preliminaries being settled, according to the established etiquette of the bull ring—the fees of entry being paid, and every incumbrance stripped off, the brave-looking bitch went in most gaily and gallantly, and immediately began to—nibble the bull's horns. We were of course bit, and somewhat chagrined. The old blade skrewed up his mug into a most excruciating smile of triumph, and fixing his squinting corkscrew glances upon our right pocket, put forth his palm for the indispensable. The bitch was terribly gored, and would not face the old bull's prickers again.

He had now been a considerable time at play, and almost every dog on the sod had tried his teeth upon him without any ultimate effect. His tough muzzle was very much lacerated, and the blood trickled down his cheeks in several distinct streams, from sundry deep bites which he had received about the eye. There was a cessation of hostilities for above four minutes. The owners of the untried dogs seemed half afraid to let them loose. Those who had been pierced were under the hands of their friends and admirers, having their gore staunched and their wounds sewed up. At last a crippled white bitch, at the command of an old butcher, by whose side she had hitherto been standing, (calmly watching the flight of the numerous dogs in the air, and the clever and effective motions of the old bull), slowly hobbled into the ring; she was covered with scars, blind in an eye, and altogether deprived of the use of one of her hind legs. Unlike many good dogs we had before seen, she did not run directly up to the bull's front, but sneaked cautiously round him, with her remaining eye vigilantly bent upon his every motion, and apparently watching for an opportunity to bolt in for a grab. This was rather *unbull-dog-like* behaviour, we must say; but when we consider the infirmity of the old bitch, and the little chance of success she would have in running in like a strong, fleet, and unmaimed dog, it may in some measure be excused. 'Tis very certain that she had pinned this same formidable bull above a dozen times, and we were informed (by a person to whose assertion we are inclined to give the most implicit credence) that she and the bull had slept many a night together in the same stall. In the stable they were as amicable as doves, but on the turf it was very different. The bull's fiery and bloodshot eye was fixed upon her the moment she made her appearance. He seems to be perfectly aware of her tremendous qualifications, and steadily kept his front towards her, turning as she turned; and disregarding all other objects, kept his keen optics fixed on her alone. Another dog unexpectedly burst into the ring while the two quadrupeds were thus steadily eyeing each other, but the bull sent him curvetting and gamboling over the heads of the spectators, without deigning (or perhaps daring) to honour him with a momentary glance. It was some time before an opportunity occurred for the bitch to get in. At length she suddenly darted forwards with a velocity of which we had deemed her incapable, and at one bound reached the bull's nose. On this occasion, however, she was unsuccessful. Her sturdy old friend tossed her off several times; but her disasters only tended to prove her invincible courage. She repeatedly went into the old bull; and at one time contrived to evade his horns so cleverly, and grappled with him so stoutly, that she would, in our opinion, eventually have pinned him, had he not trod her off by main force, and running clean over her maimed body, left her to be picked up by her fond old master.

After another irregular and very short contest, with a few fresh dogs, the particulars of which we do not remember, the bull had a very protracted breathing-time, and he was just about to be led off the ground unpinned, when a lanky, wire-haired, dingy-red coloured dog was brought to the extremity of the circle. His head was more like a lurcher's than a bull-dog's, and his tail short, thick, and rather rough and brushy. A loud laugh arose from all sides of the ring, as soon as he was introduced: a thousand fingers were pointed in derision at the dog and his master; and the old fellow with the gimblet eye once more turned up his head, and in a most unsupportable tone of voice tauntingly said, "he supposed we would even put our money upon this cur too." The circumstances of our former defeat were still fresh in our memory. We had not an atom of faith in the long spiry snipe-nosed dog—there were no symptoms of pugnacity about him; but the old joker's look and tone were a great deal too much for our philosophy. Win or lose, we were determined to bet with him; and bet we did, to the same amount and at the same odds as before, and (we still chuckle with glee to think of it) we actually won! The ugly lurcher-looking beast went resolutely up to his beef, and, without encountering a single repulse, effected a fine full-mouthed hold on the bull's snout! It was altogether miraculous and unaccountable. The enraged bull tried all his old arts to disengage himself from the dog's gripe: he tossed him furiously upwards against his keen horns, beat him from side to side tremendously on the ground, trampled on him, gallopped round the ring, lay down, rose up again in an instant, bellowed with vexation, pain, and fury, renewed the dreadful beating, trampling, and tossing; but it was all to no purpose— the ugly mongrel-looking dog stuck to him with a most inconceivable and matchless pertinacity; and at length the old bull reluctantly gave in, and suffered himself to be quietly led round the ring by his brave but plain-looking conqueror. So much for externals!

———————

P.S. Jack Cabbage (who, we were told, would not certainly buff with a friend) did not exhibit; but we had the usual quota of bouts at fisty cuffs. They manage these matters famously in the West. They don't jaw and palaver like the cockneys. "A word and a blow" is their motto: "if thee't fight I, I'll fight thee;" and a monosyllabic response in the affirmative has been the sole prelude to many a sturdy fray among the stout Bristolians. Our best wishes to them all.

———————o◯o———————

Sagacity of the Hedge-Hog. During the summer of 1818, as Mr. Lane, gamekeeper to the Earl of Galloway, was passing by the wood of Calscadden, near Garliestown, in Scotland, he fell in with a hedge-hog, crossing the road at a small distance before him, carrying on its back six pheasant's eggs, which, upon examination, he found it had pilfered from a pheasant's nest hard by. The ingenuity of the creature was very conspicuous, as several of the remaining eggs were holed, which must have been done by it, when in the act of rolling itself over the nest, in order to make as many adhere to its prickles as

possible. After watching the motions of the urchin for a short time longer, Mr. Lane saw it deliberately crawl into a furze bush, where its nest was, and where the shells of several eggs were strewed around, which had, at some former period, been conveyed thither in the same manner.

Another instance of the sagacity of the hedge-hog is also recorded by *Plutarch*. A citizen of Cyzicus formerly acquired the reputation of a good mathematician, for having learned the property of a hedge-hog. It has its burrows open in divers places, and to several winds; and foreseeing the change of the wind, stops the hole on that side; which that citizen perceiving, gave the city certain predictions to what corner the wind would shift next."

𝕸𝖊𝖒𝖔𝖎𝖗𝖘

OF

JACK SLACK.

———

E was rendered a pugilist of some prominency, by his victory over Broughton, and in being elevated to the rank of Champion!—He was a man of considerable strength and bottom; firmly made; in height about five feet eight inches and a half, and in weight nearly as heavy as Broughton, but not quite fourteen stone. *Slack* was very little indebted to science, and trusted to a method almost exclusively his own; his blows were generally well put in, and given with a most dreadful force. His attitudes were by no means impressive; there was a want of elegance in his positions to attract the attention of the spectators, and he appeared as a most determined fighter, scarcely giving time to his adversary to breathe, and bent upon nothing else but victory. He stood remarkably upright, guarding his stomach with his right hand, and as if protecting his mouth with his left. Whenever *Slack* meditated giving a blow upon any particular part of his antagonist, he rushed in furiously, regardless of the consequences of a knock-down blow in the attempt. It is but justice to say of him, that he disputed every battle manfully; was above shifting; and his bottom was of the first quality. *Slack* was noted for a back-handed blow, which often operated most powerfully upon the face of his opponent; and it was observed, that being so used to chopping in his business as a butcher, that in fighting, the chopper proved of no little service to him in producing victory.

Slack's first battle of note was with George Taylor, in 1750; but the superior science of George rendered his ferocity unavailing; and *Slack*, after a severe contest of near thirty minutes, was obliged to own he had got enough. It was a battle

[109]

spoken highly of by the sporting men of that day, for a prime
display of science and bottom.

After Broughton's defeat—Pugilism in the metropolis was
done up; and a period of upwards of four years elapsed before
a battle of any consequence took place, and then it was fought
in the country, between one Pettit, a Frenchman, and *Slack*,
at Harleston in Norfolk, in 1754.

This battle proved as singular a conflict as ever took place
in the annals of pugilism: Monsieur, on the first set-to, darted
with uncommon fury at *Slack*, and seized him by the throat,
and, for half a minute, held him tight against the rails, till
Slack was nearly choked and black in the face; and it was
with some difficulty that *Slack* released himself from this unpleasant situation. The next ten minutes the Frenchman appeared like a blacksmith hammering away at *Slack*, and driving him all over the stage with uncommon impetuosity, till at
length *Slack* closed upon Pettit, and gave him three desperate
falls; but, during which period he canted *Slack* twice off the
stage. Monsieur began to appear shy of *Slack's* method of
throwing, and ran in upon the latter and seized him by the
hams—and tumbled him down, by which means *Slack* fell easy.
A guinea to a shilling was the odds against *Slack* after they had
been fighting eighteen minutes; when, at the commencement
of the fight it was four to one in his favour. *Slack* now changed
his method of attack, and followed the Frenchman up so close,
that he had no opportunity of running in at him, but was compelled to stand up and fight; when *Slack* closed one of his eyes,
and disfigured his face in a shocking manner. Pettit's wind
now began to fail him, and *Slack* was recovering his strength
fast, when the odds were shifting rapidly on his side. Pettit,
once more got a little advantage and threw *Slack* over the rails;
but, in going over, *Slack* put in a desperate blow under the ribs
of the Frenchman, that made him cry peccavi. *Slack* was not
long in mounting the stage; but Monsieur was so panic struck,
that he brushed off with all the haste imaginable, never stopping to look back after his opponent. It was the opinion of the
spectators that Pettit was full strong when he bolted. The
battle lasted twenty-five minutes, perfectly ridiculous at times,

and equally dreadful by turns. The Frenchman not returning
to finish the contest, *Slack* was declared the conqueror, and
drew the first ten guineas out of the box.

About a twelvemonth after this fight, one Cornelius Harris,
a collier from Bristol, challenged *Slack* for one hundred guineas. Harris proved himself a good bit of stuff, teased the champion a great deal, and disputed the ground manfully; but
Slack's experience was too much for him, and, after a severe
set-to for twenty minutes, Harris gave in.

Slack now lay by in peace for upwards of four years, till one
Morton of Acton-Wells, had the temerity to call the champion
out to the field of honour, for fifty pounds. *Slack* accepted the
challenge with alacrity, and the moment of decision arrived,
when Morton shewed himself a good bottom man, and kept
the game alive for thirty-five minutes, in a style of great ex-
cellence. *Slack* had his work to do; but ultimately was declared
the victor.

Ten years had now elapsed since *Slack* had vanquished the
renowned Broughton, and held the title of champion—but the
honour was dazzling, and another hero put in his claim for
the towering prize. *Slack's* fame was well established; and here
royalty was once more busy in the pugilistic scene, by Broughton's old patron, the duke of Cumberland, stepping forward
and backing him for one hundred pounds against one Bill
Stevens, a nailer, whom the duke of York took under his patronage. The Haymarket was the scene of action, and a stage
was erected in the Tennis Court, James Street. *Slack* entered
the field with all the confidence of a veteran, and was ac-
knowleged to have the advantage in the first part of the battle;
but the nailer, with an arm like iron, received the ponderous
blows of his antagonist on his left with ease, while with his
right arm he so punished the champion's nob, that he knocked
off the title—picked it up and wore it!—Thus fell the hitherto
mighty *Slack*.

Slack now returned to his business as a butcher, and opened
a shop in that line near Covent Garden; and, being a public
man, the curiosity of the people in going to see a great fighter,
brought him considerable custom. *Slack* had a number of ac-

cidental skirmishes in his visits to fairs and other places of amusement, and was fond of what he termed—"giving the natives a small taste;" but at a country fair, affronting (what is now styled) a Johnny Raw, he, on the impulse of the moment gave the champion for his bit of fun, a prime lick on the smeller, which rather disconcerted *Slack* who thinking he had got a mere plaything, immediately put in one of his best hits as a finisher; but he was mistaken, and a regular set-to commenced. Johnny Raw, being a fine athletic young man, with plenty of pluck, fell upon *Slack* as if he had been threshing corn, and positively would have soon served out the champion—but *Slack*, now perceiving that he had picked up a troublesome customer, resorted to the following manœuvre, by way of intimidating Johnny, and cried out, with some degree of emphasis, "What! a chaw-bacon attempt to beat *Jack Slack!*" This stratagem had the desired effect upon the nerves of the unsuspecting countryman, who simply thought it impossible that he should be able to conquer so renowned a hero, exclaimed—"Dang it, what have I been fiten with that noted mon *Slack*—no, no, I woant have no more to do with he!" and instantly gave up the contest, though, in all probability, *Slack* would have been drubbed most soundly;

The above anecdote reminds us of a number of similar circumstances, (which have induced us to offer the following remarks, with the most friendly intention, trusting they may operate as a useful hint in future), that have taken place at various times, occasioned by wanton, foolish young men, who, being in possession of considerable strength, and know how to fight a little, (and even some celebrated Pugilists, who ought to have known better), have been guilty of taking up liquor in strange company, and drink of that which has not belonged to them, merely, as it is termed, for a lark; and which upon being resented as a most gross affront, by the persons who have been thus insulted, from their not being able to contend with such powerful opponents have frequently got beaten in the bargain. Such acts are most grievous indeed, and consequently bring pugilism into disgrace; but surely men, who are gifted with only a trifling share of common sense, must be well aware, that such conduct is truly despicable; and if they have the smallest intention of being respected in society, they will never take such unwarrantable liberties, in sporting with the feelings of the harmless and unoffending stranger. No Englishman will passively put up with such treatment— so derogatory to the character of a Briton!

We cannot conclude, however, without remarking that there are some men whose actions have proved them to possess feelings both of humanity, charity, and forbearance. The following anecdotes will attest the truth of this assertion. Cribb, in passing through Fore Street, Cripplegate, was most grossly insulted by a Jew of the name of Simmonds, who, valuing himself upon his manhood, and not knowing whom he was in company with, endeavoured to give him a facer; the champion, with the utmost composure, seized on this son of Mordicai, yet disdaining to inflict that sort of punishment which, in all probability must have nearly annihilated the presuming Israelite, but, instead of which, he instantly compelled him to go before the Lord Mayor, to answer for the assault. His Lordship, on hearing the case, was struck with the magnanimity displayed by Cribb on this occasion, and highly praised him for manliness of temper,—at the same time reprimanding the Jew severely for his improper behaviour. He was, however, discharged on paying the costs, to which decision the Champion, with much good nature, immediately acquiesced.

Another instance of Cribb, which is related of him during his training in Scotland previous to his battle with Molineaux, reflects the highest honor on his character. While walking along Union Street, in Aberdeen, he was accosted by a woman apparently in great distress. Her story affected him, and the emotions of his heart became evident in the muscles of his face. He gave her all the silver he had in his pocket. 'God bless your honor,' said she; 'ye surely are not an ordinary man!' This circumstance we mention with pleasure, to shew an instance, at least, in opposition to a mistaken opinion, that professional pugilists are ferocious, and totally destitute of the better propensities of mankind. The illustrious Mr. Wyndham enter-

tained juster sentiments of the pugilistic art, as evinced by a print he presented to Mr. Jackson, as a mark of his esteem. In one compartment, an Italian darting his stiletto at his victim is represented; and in the other, the combat of two Englishmen in a ring. For that celebrated genius was of opinion, that nothing tended more to preserve among the English peasantry those sentiments of good faith and honor which have ever distinguished them from the natives of Italy and Spain, than the frequent practice of fair and open Boxing.

> "Oh! 'tis excellent
> To have a giant's strength; but it is *tyrannous*
> *To use it like* a Giant.

MISCELLANEOUS.

BADGER BAITING . . . *Westminster Pit.*

No less than four badgers, in full fur, were *baited*, by four bitches, at this well-contrived arena of natural philosophy, one evening lately; besides the promise of more fun, and the equally *splendid* display, *in the bills*, of "a large baboon, the property of Capt. L—————, who (was said to have) brought it all the way from abroad, and placed great store by him."

We must not, however, suffer ourselves to be led away by the splendid promises, which could not possibly be realised in this "baboon of Capt. L. excelling the celebrated Hoxton monkey, Jacco Maccaco." Never was a more palpable blunder than this comparison: hope promised to the ear but broken to the heart; 'broken,' indeed! For our hearts were nearly rent at the cries the child-like cries of this poor little innocent-looking monkey, attacked by a bitch which had proved herself an overmatch for a more formidable animal, during a tussle of 17 minutes. Let not such *essays* be made in *public* hereafter, and this afflicted poor devil be consigned to the care of its Italian owner, and the more appropriate *office* of hopping from post to pillar for the amusement of fair-going apprentices and the admiration of their doxies.

The entertainments, although announced for seven, did not commence until past eight o'clock, when Duck-lane blazed with torch-light; but, as our readers in general may be still unacquainted with this remote '*menagerie*,' and 'tis scarcely worth a walk from 'the neighbourhood of Change' to have a sight of it.—we must be excused for obtruding a word or two concerning *the building*, and its purposes. More especially will this be desirable, inasmuch as we shall have occasion (we understand) to recur tolerably often to 'the sports' *here promised to the Fancy* during the ensuing summer. 'Tis professedly a *cock-pit* capable of containing, round the area and gallery over, an auditory of two hundred persons; apparently 18 feet long, 18 wide, and 18 high from the floor to the roof, it might notwithstanding hold a greater number of less fractious customers. Its governor and caterer is a man of professions, and a good one at making out the *bill of fare*, though utterly careless of *serving up* the promised treat; of both which we have good proof in this baboon business so largely puffed, and finally the industrious circulation, through the place of the intelligence that no monkey would be produced.

After a good deal of ogling, during which Mr. Boys was requested, but declined the honor, of being umpire in the affair. Mr. Cribb was nominated to that important post, though he previously declared he 'knew nothing of the matter;' and this act of condescension was marked by his moving to a distinguished seat below, with a *stop-watch* in his fist, which some careless person had brought with him. The stake was a silver collar to the owner of that dog which should stay longest with its game, *dead or alive.*

Badger No. 1, was a fresh one, that did not seem down to half the manœuvres necessary for its preservation; it showed no play, became currish, placing its head between its paws, and bolting from side to side the whole length of its *tether*, which was too long by half. A little white bitch played it well for 17 minutes 24 seconds, never relaxing the fight for the first 12 minutes, and then only taking, for one minute at a time, two shy breathings, when the badger seemed pleased to rest also.

No. 2, being tethered somewhat shorter, was mangled a little by a liver and white bitch, longer on the legs than the former, but a very cur. She stayed with the badger 15 minutes 21 seconds, chiefly yapping at the varment, but afraid to go in.

No. 3, was a better fight, indisputably, but nothing like murder; the badger, an old one, had less string than either of the former, brought blood from the bitch's face, and cowed his antagonist in 13 minutes and a half.

No. 4, was roused from his drowsiness by a brindled bitch, that would have found a better match in No. 3, for she was heavier than any of the others (upwards of thirty pounds), and having a good deal of the bull-dog in her breed. With these advantages, and the circumstances that this varment had not more than ten inches of string from its tail to the *ring*, gave all the preponderance of this *fourth* contest to the canine species, and 'tis not to be wondered at that she stopped 17 minutes 50 seconds. "Ten pounds that your bitch does not stay 25 minutes," was heard with apathy by her owner, and he turned a deaf ear also to the recommendation of his friends to "fight on."

This bitch took no care whatever of her feet, but went jollily to work; *her* with No. 2 literally shoved off the badger's head while he *held* her; and if we were to adjudge the prize by real *fighting*, or any thing but *time*, the white bitch with No. 3 should *have it*, beyond the world, and we should then *place them* thus, 3, 1, 4, 2.

Bill Bowser, the Oxford Jarvy, went into the pit with No. 2, and his twin-

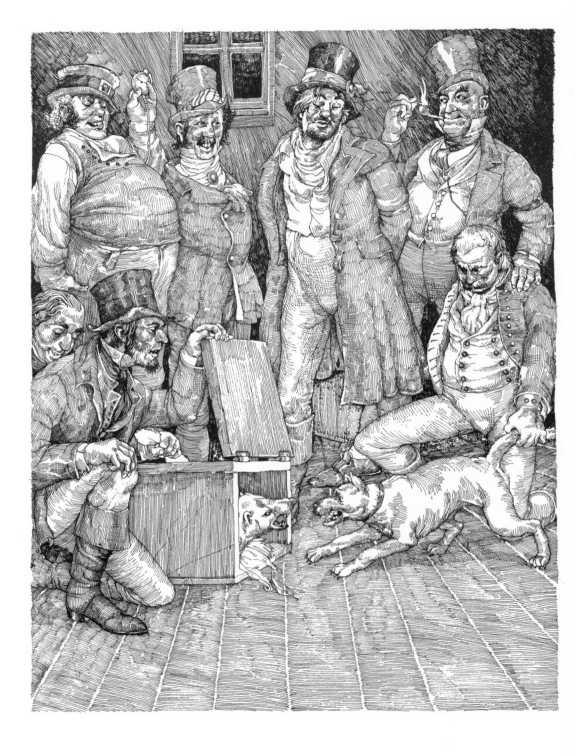

brother with No. 3! they were very properly silent with their dogs; nor until these seemed a little exhausted did we notice one "halloo." The dogs with No. 1, 2, and 3, were ill-used, in regard to shortening the tether less and less every time: and we beg leave to suggest some rule as to the length of the cord in future; as also the dastardliness of permitting some dogs to stand barking out their time, whilst one which may have killed the badger, and *gone off* in consequence of its work being completed, would be declared a loser according to the present imperfect system of adjudging the prize: what is more conclusive, the bitch with No. 4 was entangled in the string five minutes, and could not though she would get away, so there she stood panting till a fresh halloo roused both bitch and badger to fresh action.

Fourteen shillings had been paid to its owner for the loan of the first bitch; and Mr. Charles Boston very good-naturedly stood a good deal of chaffing in consequence of his making too sure of his dog being a winner.

A dog-fight was knocked up, as appears, in lieu of the monkey's performances, if that exchange could have been effected, unhappily for the cause of humanity: and however our national characteristic for *manliness* towards all the creatures of God's creation, viz. let the brutes have their way, but do not pair them against the rules of nature. But of this animal we shall say no more: for although occurring the last upon the bill, our indignation brought that subject uppermost, like the rankling of an old grudge.

Cato, a powerful dog, mostly liver-coloured, fought in good style his more cunning antagonist Turpin; this latter, having a fawn-coloured coat, less weight, and fighting underneath, was a long while in showing his tactics to advantage. He however made the proper impression in a quarter of an hour, by constantly holding the throat of Mr. Cato, who sought to bolt in that time, and was with difficulty prevailed upon to go in once more, and take a taste additional as a kind of farewell bite. The sports at this place occur weekly: but are not in general worth notice.

————o◯o————

The Inspired Gamester.—An Archbishop of Canterbury making a tour into the country, stopped at an Inn for refreshment. Being at the window, he observed at a distance, in a solitary wood, a well-dressed man alone, talking, and acting a kind of part.

The prelate's curiosity was excited, to know what the stranger was about, and he accordingly sent some of his servants to observe him, and hear what he was rehearsing. But they bringing back an answer far from satisfactory, his Grace resolved to go himself; he accordingly repaired to the wood, ordering his attendant to keep at a distance. He addressed the stranger very politely, and was answered with the same civility. A conversation having been once entered into though not without interruptions, by an occasional soliloquy, his grace asked what he was about. "I am at play," he replied. "At play," said the prelate, "and with whom? you are all alone!" "I own," said he, "Sir, you do not perceive my antagonist, but I am playing with God." "Playing with

God!" (his lordship thinking the man out of his mind), this is a very extraordinary party; and pray at what game, Sir, are you playing?" "At chess, Sir." The Archbishop smiled; but the man seeming peaceable, he was willing to amuse himself with a few more questions. "And do you play for any thing, sir?" "Certainly." "You cannot have any great chance, as your adversary must be so superior to you!" "He does not take any advantage, but plays merely like a man." "Pray, Sir; when you win or lose, how do you settle your accounts?" "Very exactly and punctually, I promise you." "Indeed! pray how stands your game?" The stranger, after muttering something to himself, said, "I have just lost it." "And how much have you lost?" "Fifty guineas." "That is a great sum; how do you intend paying it, does God take your money?" "No, the poor are his treasurers; he always sends some worthy person to receive the debt, you are at present the purse-bearer." Saying this, he pulled out his purse, and counting fifty guineas, put them into his grace's hand, and retired saying, "He should play no more that day."

The prelate was quite fascinated: he did not know what to make of this extraordinary adventure, he viewed the money, and found all the guineas good; recalled all that had passed, and began to think there must be something in this man more than he had discovered. However, he continued his journey, and applied the money to the use of the poor, as he had been directed.

Upon his return he stopped at the same inn, and perceiving the same person again in the wood, in his former situation, he resolved to have a little further conversation with him, and went alone to the spot where he was. The stranger was a comely man and the prelate could not help viewing him with a kind of religious veneration, thinking, by this time, that he was inspired to do good in this uncommon manner. The prelate accosted him as an old acquaintance and familiarly asked him how the chance stood since they had last met. "Sometimes for me, and sometimes against me; I have both lost and won." "And are you at play now?" "Yes, Sir, we have played several games to day." "And who wins?" "Why Sir at present the advantage is on my side, the game is just over, I have a fine stroke; check mate, there it is." "And pray Sir, how much have you won?" "Five hundred guineas!" "That is a handsome sum; but how are you to be paid?" "I pay and receive in the like manner: he always sends me some good rich man when I win; and you my lord, are the person. God is remarkably punctual upon these occasions."

The Archbishop had received a very considerable sum on that day: the stranger knew it, and produced a pistol by way of a receipt; the prelate found himself under the necessity of delivering up his cash; and, by this time, discovered the divine inspired gamester to be neither more nor less than a thief. His Lordship had, in the course of his journey related the first part of this adventure, but the latter part he prudently took great pains to conceal.

Fight between a Lion and three Mastiffs.—John Stow, in his Annals, has an account of a battle between three mastiffs and a lion, in the presence of James

the First and his son, prince Henry. "One of the dogs being put into the den, was soon disabled by the lion, which took him by the head and neck, and dragged him about. Another dog was then let loose, and served in the same manner; but the third being put in immediately, seized the lion by the lip, and held him for a considerable time; till being severely torn by his claws, the dog was obliged to quit his hold; and the lion, greatly exhausted by the conflict, refused to renew the engagement; but, taking a sudden leap over the dogs, fled into the interior part of his den. Two of the dogs soon died of their wounds; the third survived, and was taken great care of by the prince, who said, "he that had fought with the king of beasts, should never after fight with an inferior creature."

DESCRIPTION OF A MODERN MILL,

*Said to have taken place between Big Barney, a trowel-tosser & labourer,
and Surly Sam, a Birmingham bellows blower.*

I send you, friend Bob, bitter moments to sweeten,
An account how Big Barney by Surly was beaten.
This *mill*, long expected, was last week decided,
About which the FANCY were so much divided.
Costermongers in *drags* went to witness the slaughter,
And *Corinthian swells* of the very first water.
The odds *six to four* when the combatants started,
But the *backers* were *down*—'ere ten minutes departed.
When *peel'd*, Barney seem'd in high twig and condition,
And as supple as if dipp'd in *Anti-attrition!*
But Sam *floor'd* him the moment he came to the *scratch*,
And twisted his *mauley's* 'mongst Goliah's *thatch*.
Then he *mill'd* him and *fib'd* him beyond his friends' hopes,
And threw him, like winking, right over the ropes;
Next he starr'd Magog's *glaze*, and well scuttl'd his nob,
To the joy of Tom Cribb, at a mill—the Nabob.
Surly's blows at his *list'ner* at length made him cringe,
For they folded him up like an old rusty binge.
Barney's backers looked *peery* while losing their *rag*—
'Twas all Holywell-street to an old clothes-man's bag:
Tho' beat to a stand still, he yet display'd game,
'Till the ring echoed loud, "*choak him off; 'tis a shame!*"
In short, 'twas remark'd by GAS, RANDALL, and SUTTON,
That they never before had beheld such a GLUTTON!
Beat almost out of time, quite abroad in the garret,
His power exhausted, the ring dy'd with claret.
He still came to the *scratch* to receive Surly's knocks,

Which remov'd all the *tools* from his *domino-box;*
He at last was so punish'd and queer'd in the crummy,
Hit as black as a *hearse*, and quite *weav'd* to a mummy;
With his *daylights* stopp'd up, to his man he was led,
His *head-rails* displac'd, and in *chanc'ry* his head;
Bor'd senseless, beat stupid, and quite on the pot,
He receiv'd Surly's *"fives,"* and went down like a shot;
Where he lay as *entranc'd*, doubled up like a letter,
From whence he was borne to a *drag* on a shutter.
The fight lasted, by those who by stop-watches reckon'd,
One hour, ten minutes, a half, and one second!

Chaffing Crib, Corinthian Hall,
    April 27, 1822.

_____

The Rival Combatants.—Mr. *J. T. C.* appeared in custody before the bench at Hatton Garden, on a warrant charging him with having assaulted and beaten one Mr. *Richard Arnold Alexander*, against the peace of our sovereign lord the king, his crown and dignity.

Mr. *C.* is a very personable looking young man, gentlemanly in his manners, of highly respectable connexions, and very sanguine temperament—at times, indeed, approaching to the choleric. Mr. *Richard Arnold Alexander*, on the contrary, is a man of vulgar exterior, well stricken in years, his short, round, shining countenance of a bright scarlet, inclining to orange, topped with a trifle of lank grisly hair, and his sinister arm shrivelled up to less than half its natural size; and yet the cause of their quarrel was a very pretty young woman —one Miss *Hannah Juliana Fidkins*, who, in the free exercise of her taste and judgment, had deserted the young man for the old one.

It appeared by the old gentleman's statement, however, that as he was walking along Hatton Garden on Sunday afternoon, with Miss *Juliana Fidkins* hanging on his arm, he was aware of the young gentleman coming towards him; and well aware that he was coming with no peaceful intent, he cautioned him to keep his distance. But the young gentleman, totally disregarding the caution, came boldly up in front, and, having called him an old scoundrel, instantly knocked him down with a blow on the face, that made his very eyes strike fire. The old gentleman, finding himself on the ground, gathered himself up as soon as he could, and, having regained his perpendicular, he found the young gentleman in an attitude for flooring him a second time; but he, having no relish for such flooring, endeavoured to defend himself with a little bit of stick he had in his hand. The young gentleman, however, was too quick for him, and, in spite of his utmost endeavours, and those of Miss *Juliana Fidkins* to boot, he was again knocked down, and soundly beaten with his own stick.

This was the case for the prosecution, and it was fully substantiated by Miss *Juliana Fidkins*; who thumping her little white fist on the table, in-

veighed bitterly against the persecutions she had endured from the young gentleman, because she had thought proper to place herself 'under the protection' of the old one.

The young gentleman, on the other hand, retorted, with equal bitterness, the falsehood and the ingratitude of Miss *Juliana Fidkins*; and he seemed to feel what he uttered. With respect to the assault, he denied that he was the aggressor, though 'he had savage cause;' and he insisted that it was Miss *Juliana Fidkins* herself who began the affray, by running after him and demanding a parasol of her's which he had in his possession. He was, at the time, going quietly to the evening service at St. Andrew's Church, and was much vexed at having his passions disturbed by meeting with the 'old villain and his paramour.' He consequently put her gently by with his arm, and requested her to let him pass in peace: but he *had hardly opened his mouth* when the old gentleman came up 'like a strutting old turkey-cock,' and seized him by the collar. He instantly shook off the contaminating grasp of the 'hoary dotard,' and he tumbled on the ground. Miss *Fidkins* picked him up again, and it was then that the 'bit of a stick,' the 'old fool' had spoken of, came into play; but that *bit of a stick*, he declared, was as thick as a man's arm, and had a knob at the end of it three times as large as his fist! With this neat little switch, the 'old man' was no sooner placed on his feet than he began laying on him with all his might; and he, therefore, wrested it from him and threw it into the middle of the street, and in the scuffle, the old man again tumbled down.

This he declared was a true statement of the business, and he called a witness who corroborated it in almost every particular; and deposed, not only to the immense size of the stick, but also to his having seen the old gentleman give the young one three distinct blows with it on the 'seat of honour,' before he turned about to resent it.

The magistrate having listened to these contradictory statements with most exemplary patience, seemed disposed to consider the matter favourable for the younger of the lovers—indeed, he had already expressed his intention of permitting the warrant to be suspended for a few days, and letting him go at large on condition of his promising not to interfere with the old gentleman again. But only see the impetuosity of youth! His worship had scarcely given utterance to these intentions, than the young gentleman began to talk largely of his having intended to get warrants against the 'old man' and Miss *Juliana Fidkins*, for their attack upon *him*.—'Against *me*?' asked the indignant Miss *Fidkins*.—'Yes, against *you*! you *hussy*!' replied the luckless lover; and he had no sooner said so, than his worship ordered that he should find bail for his appearance at the quarter-sessions, as it was very evident he was a very violent young man. If he is wise, he will never again 'hoot before he is out of the wood.'

Matters being thus settled, the forlorn swain retired in custody to send for bail; and the venerable and favored lover, with Miss *Hannah Juliana Fidkins* on his arm, withdrew as comfortable as possible.

𝔐𝔢𝔪𝔬𝔦𝔯𝔰

OF

JOSHUA HUDSON.

———

THE above *handy* hero with his *"bunch of fives,"* first fought his way into the world at Rotherhithe, on the 21st of April, 1797. He was a *gay* boy almost from his cradle; and has had as many *turn-ups* and street *sets-to,* by way of *practice*, as any of the fighting men on the list. In the neighbourhood of Rotherhithe, and down the road, were the principal scenes of action in which *Josh.* obtained much *notoriety.* Yet, although fond of *milling* to the echo, and always ready to be *matched,* there is a great deal of the Englishman about his character for *humanity. Ferocity* does not belong to his composition: but in the fight he is *terrific. Hudson* will not be denied; and he is a *glutton* of the first appetite. He has an open, nay, a good-natured countenance. He is fond of what the sailors call a *"a shindy;"* and, indeed, the most prominent traits of a Jack Tar are to be witnessed about *Joshua Hudson.* He does not want for information; and when the *grog* is not on board, he is truly inoffensive in his disposition. He is in weight from 11 stone 8 lbs. to 12 stone; in height about 5 feet 8 inches. *Josh.* if not a first-rate scientific fighter, does not want for excellent skill. He is a hard hitter with both hands, but he uses the right to the most advantage. He is cool and steady when in battle. *Hudson* is a pupil of *Tom Owen;* and, under his guidance, he has fought all his contests of note.

The first regular contest in which *Josh.* displayed his *milling talent* for a prize was with *Jack the Butcher,* at Dartford Brim, on October the 22, 1816, for 10 guineas a side. *Jack,* if he *liked* it, could fight well and hit hard; more especially, if he thought victory was within his grasp; but, if he lost the *lead,* his *pluck* evaporated, as it were, and he did not care how soon the battle was over. However, *Jack* thought he could take the *shine* out of his opponent in this contest, and fought tolerably well: but *Hudson* was too gay and too *game* for his adversary, and in 35 minutes *Josh.* was declared the conqueror.

Our hero now entered the lists with *Abraham Belasco*, the Jew, at Barge House, Woolwich. It was a most determined battle for one hour and thirty minutes. It, however, ended in a *wrangle*; both of the combatants claiming the money. *Clark* and *Warren* seconded *Josh.*

Hudson's next battle was with *Street*, April 5, 1817. *Josh.* won this fight in one hour and ten minutes. The smiles of victory also crowned his efforts for a purse of 10 guineas, in his battle with *Charley Martin*, at Sawbridgeworth, on June 10, 1817, in half an hour.

Hudson, who it appears, had a great aversion to be idle, was matched with one *Thompson*, for 10 guineas a side, in less than six weeks after the above contest. It was considered a good battle; but *Hudson* won it in prime style, in the short space of 25 minutes.

The lively disposition of our hero has led him into too many *freaks*, and, owing to some row, he was bound over to keep the peace, in a heavy bond, for 12 months. His friends, to render this *"peace keeping"* more certain on the part of *Josh.* prevailed on him to take a voyage to the East Indies. *Hudson* embraced the idea with great pleasure, and he accordingly went on board the *Surat Castle*, Indiaman, for Bombay, in the capacity of the ship butcher. But having too great an allowance of *grog*, and not *relishing* the *chaffing* of the second mate, *Mr. Bishop*, *Josh.* in an intemperate moment, made use of his *morleys* upon the *nob* of the mate, and our hero was, in consequence, put in irons for three weeks, and his legs stapled to the deck, as a punishment for his offence, and a sentinel ordered to do duty over him.

Hudson, to keep his *hand* in, took a turn with one *M'Carthy*, between decks, at Gravesend. The latter could fight a "little bit," and backed himself for two months' advance. In the course of three rounds poor *M'Carthy napt* it so severely, as to be glad to *sing* out for quarter.

During the time *Hudson* was at Bombay, he had a "few

words" with *Tom Bryant*, who was viewed as the terror of
the crew, on board the *Surat*. In the cable tier, *Hudson* and
Bryant had a most determined fight; but in the course of a
quarter of an hour, the latter boxer was so severely *punished*,
that he admitted *Josh.* was the best man. *Bryant* and *Hudson*
were sworn friends ever afterwards.

Our hero had not long returned to old England, when, it
should seem, under the idea that he might lose the proper use
of his *hands*, if he did not have plenty of practice, *Josh.* without
any consideration or hesitation on the subject, agreed to fight
Bowen, a caulker, 6 feet 2 inches in height, and weighing 13
stone 6 lbs. on March 25, 1819. This man was denominated
the Champion of Chatham. Indeed, it was a *horse* to a *hen*;
Hudson only weighing 10 stone 7 lbs. But, notwithstanding
this great disparagement of size and weight, *Josh.* fought like
a *trump*, and contended for the victory for 35 minutes, till he
had not a leg to stand upon.

It will be seen, that *Josh.* lost no time in endeavouring to
recover from the chilling effects of his late defeat, and was
matched, on Tuesday, April 27, 1819, against *Williams*, a
waterman, for 10 guineas aside, near the sign of the Prince
Regent, in Essex, opposite to Woolwich Warren. The day
proving fine, upwards of 5000 persons were present; but the
majority were *country folks*. *Hudson* stood high with the amateurs as a *good one*; and he was the favourite 5 to 4. At thirteen
minutes past one o'clock, *Hudson* entered the ring, attended
by his seconds, *Owen* and *Donelly*; and *Williams* was also followed by *Oliver* and *Holt*. The first three rounds were in favour of the *Waterman*, and in closing both down. But, from
the activity and superior hitting of *Hudson*, a change was soon
effected; and, towards the end of the battle, the *Waterman* had
not a *chance*. He was, on quitting the ring, completely in the
dark; punished terribly; and his chief merit consisted in his
gluttony; in fact, he was a complete *Purcell* for displaying
game. There was too much *wood-work* in his composition; however, *Hudson* did not get off without *napping* heavily. It was,
upon the whole, a very manly fight; and the amateurs seemed
to think, that *Hudson* was entitled, from the *tactics* he dis-

played, to *look out* for a *customer* of higher rank on the list than those he had yet been opposed to.

In consequence of *Boone* not appearing to fight *Kendrick*, the black, according to a previous agreement, to make the second fight at Moulsey Hurst, on Tuesday, August 24, 1819, after *Cy. Davis* and *Boshell* had left the ring, a purse of 25 guineas was made up on the ground, and *Scroggins* and *Josh. Hudson* agreed to fight for the same. *Harmer* and *Shelton* were for the former, and *Owen* and *Sutton* for *Hudson*. *Scroggins* rather hesitated, on account of his bad condition, asserting that he had been up all night, his time also been amorously employed, and full of *lush;* but said, win or lose, he would have a *shy* for it. Eleven rounds were contested occupying 18 minutes; but a short description will prove quite sufficient; *Scroggins* rushed head-long at his opponent, his eyes appearing shut, frequently running by him, scrambling to make a hit, and fell off his balance; while, on the contrary, *Hudson* was cool and collected, and *nobbed* this once *great little hero*, with *punishing* and *stupifying* effect. In the first round it was 2 to 1 on *Hudson;* in the sixth it was 15 to 5; and *Tom Owen* observed to his man, "It's all your own; you do not want any second. A few more hits, my boy, and you shall have the *pence."* It was a complete bull-dog fight, and *Scroggins* was *reeling* from the *nobbing* he had received. In the eleventh and last round, he was hit after he had fallen on his knees. "Foul, foul," "Fair, fair," Time was called, but *Scroggins* said, he had been hit unfair. The umpire was appealed to, who decided the circumstance as fair. *Scroggins* was then asked if he would fight any more? He said, "No! if they called such *usage* as he had received *fair."* The purse was then declared to be the property of *Hudson*. *Scroggins*, in the first three or four rounds of the fight, was as full of *antics* as if he had been performing the part of a clown, in a pantomine. *Hudson* was rather *distressed* in the ninth round, owing to the furious attacks of his opponent.

In consequence of a quarrel between *Josh. Hudson* and *Sampson*, the *Birmingham Youth*, who had been previously great friends, but, at this period, implacable enemies, they met together at Wallingham Common, Surrey, on Tuesday, October 26, 1819. If ever the *out-and-out* courage of an English bull-dog was witnessed, the *game* displayed by *Hudson* in some of the rounds was equal to it. In fact his *bottom* astonished all present. And it is only common justice to assert, that *Sampson* was also a brave rival in this respect.

Twenty-five rounds occurred, occupying 40 minutes, all of which were distinguished for tremendous fighting. *Hudson* received three or four *flooring* hits. Such a good fight was not often witnessed, and victory was declared in favour of *Hudson*. It was a *nice* thing, and also dearly bought, as *Hudson* fainted on his second's knee, almost the instant after he was proclaimed the conqueror.

Hudson, from the *game* and milling talents he had displayed, was matched against *Martin* for 50 guineas a side, which took place at Colnbrook, on Tuesday, December, 14, 1819, when in the second round, *Hudson*'s shoulder was dislocated, and, of course, he lost the battle.

An *off-hand* match was made for *Hudson* against *Rasher*, a determined Welshman, a butcher belonging to Whitechapel market. The latter boxer had the weight of *Josh.*; but, nevertheless, he fought *Rasher* ten guineas to eight. It occupied 29 minutes and a half, and 15 rounds. After the first round, which was tremendously contested, *Hudson* had it all his own way. The science displayed by the latter boxer was much admired; and he made feints with his left hand, to get the right well into play. *Rasher* was covered with *claret*; his *gameness* astonished every person present; but he was too *slow* in his movements. He was *floored* quite senseless in the last round; but on coming to himself, *Rasher* wanted again to renew the fight.

Hudson, still continuing to rise in the estimation of his friends, was backed, without any fear or hesitation, against *Benniworth*, the Essex Foulness Island Champion, the terror of the country for several miles round, for 50 guineas a side.

This contest took place on Tuesday April 4, 1820, on a common near Billericay, in Essex. Any description is useless. —*Hudson* had it all his own way. He laughed at *Benniworth*, and *nobbed* him at pleasure. The Essex Champion had now lost his temper, rushed in and followed *Hudson* all over the ring, with his head leaning forward, and both his hands sprawling open. *Hudson* all the time kept retreating, and jobbing his adversary on the head, with his left hand. *Benniworth* was a complete receiver-general; but, nevertheless, he succeeded in driving *Hudson* to the ropes. But here he had the worst of it, a guinea to a shilling. *Josh. nobbed* him terribly away; and, also, in following *Benniworth, Josh. floored* him with a terrific right-handed hit on his nose. The chancery suit was now complete; and *Benniworth,* when *"time"* was called, was in such a state of stupor, that he could not leave the knee of his second; when *Hudson* was declared the conqueror.

Thus was this mighty Essex Champion disposed of in the short space of *seven minutes.* But, as a scientific pugilist, *Benniworth* does not appear to possess a single point. He has no idea of fighting. From the moment he entered the ring, *Hudson* kept laughing at him; and beat him without a *scratch* upon his face. It most certainly was a very laughable, but not an interesting, contest; and it was a matter of great astonishment how *such* a boxer could have obtained so terrific a character, for miles round his native place.

Josh. was all of a sudden called into action with *Spring,* at Moulsey Hurst, on Tuesday, June 27, 1820, for a purse of £20; and, notwithstanding, the disparagement of size and weight between the combatants, *Hudson* showed himself a good man, and a boxer of talent.

Hudson, during the time he was at Norwich, had a battle with *Abraham Belasco,* in the long room, at Gurney's Bowling Green. In this contest, which might be termed for honour, *Josh.'s* shoulder went *in* and *out* three times.

Mousley Hurst, on Tuesday, December 5, 1820, was again the favourite "bit of turf" for a genteel *mill* between a *Swell* of the name of *Williams* and *Josh. Hudson. Williams* was perfectly unknown to the mass of amateurs; but those persons who knew him, or *pretended* to be acquainted with his prime fighting qualities, *chaffed* all the *ould* ring goers out of conceit of their own judgment, and *Williams* was the favourite, 6 and 5 to 4.

The *Swell* was supported and brought forward by the *Swells*. *Judgment* was shoved, as it were, into the back ground; or else a *novice* in the ring would never have been backed, at high odds, against a well-known high-couraged man; one who had often been put to the test; and also a boxer of some talent. But then the *shoulder* of *Hudson* was *ricketty*, and no dependance could be placed upon it. This is the only hole to creep out of for the bad judgment that has been displayed. However, it must be admitted, the *excuse* is not without some weight. Things went on in this manner till about a few minutes before one o'clock, *Williams* appeared, and threw his hat into the ring, followed by *Belcher* and *Randall*, as his seconds. The *look* of *Williams* was *swellish* in the extreme, and he was *togged* out accordingly. He bowed in the most graceful manner; and there was a superior air about him altogether. He paced the ring up and down for about eight minutes; when *Josh. Hudson*, with his white topper on, a prime fancy upper benjamin, a blue bird's eye *fogle* round his *squeeze*, came brushing along, and threw his *castor* into the ring. He immediately went up to *Williams*, and shook hands with him in the true open-hearted English style. *Williams* observed to *Hudson*, "that he hoped there was no animosity between them." "Not in the least," said he; "we are going to fight for a prize, and to see which is the best man." *Tom Owen* and *Ned Turner* were the seconds for *Josh. Hudson*.

First round.—On stripping, *Williams* displayed a fine muscular frame, and also good legs; but his face was very pale. His countenance bespoke that of a man between forty and fifty years of age. *Josh.* was in high trim, and he seemed confident of winning. Some time elapsed after the combatants had placed themselves in attitudes, when *Williams* let fly; but *Hudson* got away. Counter hits occurred, when *Josh.'s* right eye showed blood, and the nose of the *Swell* looked a little red. *Williams* made a right-handed hit, which *Hudson* stopped prettily, and then went to work, and the exchanges were sharp and hard; but the *wisty-castors* of *Josh.* were so tremendous, that he spoilt the gentility of the *Swell*, and *milled* him down. Great applause from the plebeians; and *Tom Owen* smilingly said to *Josh.*, "I told you so, my boy. Why that's the way to clear Regent-street of all the *Swells* in a brace of shakes."—7 to 4.

Second.—*Josh.'s* eye was bleeding when he came up to the scratch. The *Swell* was rather puzzled; but he touched *Hudson's* other *peeper* so severely, that his *mob* was *chanceried* for an instant. *Hudson* made a plunge with his right hand upon his opponent's face, that produced the *claret*; followed him up to the ropes, and punished him down.—3 to 1, and "It's poundable," was the cry. Here the Welshman told *Josh.* he had "done the trick, and *lots of daffy* were in store for him."

Third.—The hitherto genteel appearance of the *Swell* had left him, and his *mug*, it was chaffed, had paid a visit to *Pepper Alley.* *Williams* showed game, but he had no chance to win. He, however, made some sharp hits; but the *pepper-box* was again administered, and *Williams* went down quite distressed. —10 to 1.

This round was the *quietus* as to the side of winning, and the *Swell* was hit out of the ring. It was *cayenne* at every hit. *Williams* was completely *smashed*, and his seconds dragged him up all but gone.

Sixth.—*Williams* came to the scratch in the most piteous state, and he was *floored sans ceremonie.* When time was called he could not leave his second's knee.

One pill is a dose; and the *Swell* ought not to fight any more. In the short space of nine minutes he was hit all to pieces; and after remaining a short time in a state of stupor, on coming to his recollection, he asked, "if he was licked." The flash side have been completely *floored*, in consequence of their calculating upon *Josh.'s* shoulder giving way. The latter fought in fine style, and scarcely used his defective shoulder.

Shortly after, *Hudson* had rather a ridiculous turn-up with *Turner*, at a public house at the east end of the town. They were, however, separated, on the company observing that they were not fighting for a prize. *Hudson* had the worst of it.

A slight skirmish also took place between *Josh. Hudson* and *Jack Ford*, on Thursday evening, March 29, 1821, at the east end of the town, over a pot of *heavy*. *Ford* offered to fight *Dav.*

Hudson; when *Josh.* said it was cowardly to challenge a blind one. *Ford* immediately gave *Josh. a snorter,* which not only produced the *claret,* but sent his *pimple* through *three* pains of glass: *Josh.* could not return the *favour* till he had put the pot and glass out of his hand: when the *John Bull boxer* caught hold of *Ford,* and put in such a shower of hailstones on his *nob,* that he roared out for help, and begged of the company to take *Josh.* away from him, if they did not wish to see him (*Ford*) *murdered!—Josh. Hudson* offered to *accommodate Ford* any time in a public ring, if he *liked* it: but observed that he must take no more *liberties* in future with his head, in a public house; or else he must answer before the *Beak* for such conduct!—*Jack Ford,* in his day, fought some of the best men on the list: he was defeated by *Oliver* and *Harmer;* but he conquered *Harry Lancaster.*

Hudson has also distinguished himself in two battles during the present year: viz. the *Chatham Caulker,* on Wimbledon Common, on Tuesday, February 5th, which he won cleverly, in the short space of three minutes and a half; and with *Barlow,* the Yorkshireman, on the 17th of September, on the heath at St. Albans. This battle must be in the recollection of all our readers; and many that day felt the folly of backing a mere novice against a man of scientific attainment, and possessing courage not to be excelled by any man in the kingdom. These successes have made him an object of great attraction to the Fancy; and his forthcoming battle with *Shelton* is looked forward to with much interest.

Hudson is always ready to take the field; he makes no objection when any match is proposed to him, although his *shoulder* might be considered as a great drawback on his confidence: and his courage is of such high quality, that he looks forward to victory in all his contests with the utmost certainty. Such a pugilist, therefore, as *Hudson,* is not likely to remain idle. He is so anxious upon all occasions to exhibit his prowess in the Prize Ring, that he will not refuse a challenge, however much above his weight.

Nineteen hundred and fifty copies of Selections from The Fancy *have been printed for the members of the Imprint Society by The Press of A. Colish, in Mount Vernon, New York. The text was composed in English Monotype Bell. The paper is Curtis Rag laid text. The illustrations and the original etching, which is laid in, are by Randy Jones. The book was designed by Bert Clarke, and bound by Publishers Book Bindery, in Long Island City, New York.*

This is number 181

and is here signed by the artist

Randy Jones